THE ALTERNATIVE GCSE GUIDES

ENGLISH

LITERATURE

EXAM SUCCESS WITHOUT THE STRESS

GCSE GUIDES

Sherry Ashworth

Illustrated by Polly Dunbar

For Juliet Shepherd.

Sherry Ashworth is an English teacher, freelance journalist and writer of fiction for teenagers. She lives in Manchester with her husband and two daughters.

With thanks to our educational consultant, Anna Johnson.

Scholastic Children's Books,
Commonwealth House, 1-19 New Oxford Street,
London, WC1A 1NU, UK
A division of Scholastic Ltd
London - New York - Toronto - Sydney - Auckland
Mexico City - New Delhi - Hong Kong

First published in the UK by Scholastic Ltd, 2001

ISBN 0 439 99748 8

Typeset by M Rules
Printed by Cox & Wyman Ltd, Reading, Berks.

10 9 8 7 6 5 4 3 2 1

Contents

Welcome

This alternative guide is designed to lead you through the maze of English Literature GCSE. It begins by tell—

No – cut it right now. I thought this wasn't going to be an ordinary kind of textbook. I've had enough of those. All those clever clogs telling you how easy studying literature is, when anyone can tell you it's almost impossible to find the right things to say…

Or how writing essays can be mind-numbingly boring… Or how you try to read your set text at home and you realize you can't understand a word of it…

Too right!
And how do you know what quotes to use? And why isn't it good enough just to say you've enjoyed a book – why do you have to give reasons for everything?

And why do things seem obvious when the teacher explains them, but never when you're trying to work out ideas yourself?

Yes - and the most important thing - what if I don't get the final grade I need? I reckon I need someone to help me suss out Eng Lit.

You've come to the right book. It'll show you how to get the most out of your set texts, it'll dish the dirt on the tricks writers use, and you'll find out how easy it is to write brilliant essays. If you feel like giving up on Eng Lit, then read this book first. I guarantee it will change your mind.

At GCSE, English Literature is divided into three categories:

1. POETRY — anything written in verse, could be short or long, serious or funny.

2. DRAMA — plays – anything from Shakespeare to modern theatre.

3. PROSE — a mystifying word simply meaning either novels or short stories or anything else not written in verse, e.g. an autobiography or essay.

And then the examiners divide literature again into two further sections:

1. PRE-TWENTIETH CENTURY – stuff written before 1900.

2. TWENTIETH CENTURY – stuff written after 1900.

The examiners insist you read texts from both before and after 1900 so you get a feel for how English Literature has changed over the centuries.

What's your syllabus?

Every student sitting English Literature at GCSE will have a syllabus (a course of study) set by one of six examination boards. Your teacher can let you know which board's exams you're taking.

However, all the six syllabuses have elements in common:

- You sit an exam at the end of the course which is worth 70 per cent of your final mark.

- You write a coursework folder during your course worth 30 per cent of your final mark.

- You study prose, poetry and drama, both pre-1900 and post-1900.

- You must show you can compare and contrast texts.

- You must know something about the literary traditions and social and historical influences on some of the texts you study.

OK. So what exactly are (yawn!) literary traditions?

Literary tradition just means how writers wrote at the time. For instance, in Shakespeare's time, playwrights wrote mainly in verse. And in the eighteenth century nearly all poetry rhymed. Today, most plays aren't in verse and a poet can choose freely how to write his or her poetry. There are fashions in literature just like there are in everything. So if you study literature, it's cool to know what the fashions are.

8

I get it. And social and historical influences?

Social and historical influences means what was happening around the time the writer wrote. A lot of writers decide to write because they've got a point to make about the world they live in. Take Harper Lee, for example. She was born in 1925 and spent her childhood in the deep south of the USA, where there was a lot of racism. The novel she's famous for – *To Kill a Mockingbird* – is about racism, and shows the reader how subtle and terrifying it can be. You've got to know a bit about racism in the USA to get the most out of reading the novel.

But if I'm interested in racism in America, wouldn't I be better off reading factual books about it, rather than a story someone's made up?

OK. Let's say you're in your favourite record store to buy a CD. You've got two choices: the disc itself in a plain case, or the disc in a case with fold-out notes giving you the details of the group, what made them write the music, pics of their recent gigs, the lyrics etc etc. Obviously you'd buy the second. Why settle for the plain music when you can have so much more? So why settle for just the facts of a situation when literature can give you extra? By using the power of the writer's imagination, and your imagination, you get the feeling of being alive in those times, through words that express perfectly what the situation was like, a story with a beginning, middle and end, characters you can identify with—

OK, so you've made your point.

What sort of reader are you?

Before you embark on your GCSE course, it's as well to know a little bit about yourself. Try this cunningly designed quiz to see what sort of literature student you are.

1. You've got a book to read from school. You settle down in the living room to start it. After a time you…

a) go to the kitchen to see if there are any biscuits.

b) get so involved you don't notice time passing.

c) wander around the house so everyone can see the book in your hand.

d) turn on the TV and watch your favourite programme while reading simultaneously.

e) stop at one particular point because you disagree with what the writer is trying to say.

2. Your teacher has just read a poem aloud in class and asks for people's opinions on it. You…

a) start doodling in the margins of your notebook.

b) can't wait to share your thoughts with the rest of the class.

c) smile inscrutably, exchange glances with the teacher, indicating you might have something to say if she begs you.

d) tell your mate what you think.

e) don't agree with what the poet is trying to say but you don't feel like saying so because you're in a mood.

3. You're in the library looking for something to read on the fiction shelves. You…

a) end up looking out of the window because you never realized you could see the park from the library, and you wonder if your mum's there with your baby brother.

b) pick up an interesting-looking book and get so absorbed you settle down on an easy chair and get stuck in.

c) stroll over to the librarian and ask if they have anything by the latest Booker Prize-winner.

d) spot this stunning member of the opposite sex and steal glances at them while pretending to select a novel.

e) think it's a pity all the library books look so tatty and wonder if the government is spending enough on libraries.

4. It's bedtime. You snuggle up with something to read. It's…

a) a fantasy or a romance novel.

b) a long Victorian novel.

c) a bluffer's guide to English Literature.

d) your fave magazine.

e) the newspaper.

5. The worst has happened. Your lit teacher has set you an essay on your set text. You…

a) spend three hours trying to decide on the first sentence.

b) spend three hours researching and planning it.

c) spend three hours looking for your elder sister's essay on the same book.

d) spend three hours at your mate's house hanging out.

11

e) spend three hours moaning to your dad about the unfairness of homework and the examination system.

Results:

Mostly **a)**s: **The Daydreamer**. You like reading but have a tendency to drift off. Your favourite sorts of books must have a good story and you need to identify strongly with the characters. You're imaginative, sensitive and you're putting on weight because of all those biscuits in question one.

Mostly **b)**s: **The Enthusiast**. You have a passion for literature and are never happier than when your nose is in a book, and that's not just because you're hiding that new spot that's just appeared. For you Eng Lit GCSE is actually the most enjoyable GCSE of all – you can read, think about what you read and explain yourself on paper – and they call that work! You like any book, but the more challenging, the better.

Mostly **c)**s: **The Poseur**: You have a certain image to maintain, so it's important a book has the right cover. You'll quote what you read from time to time, just to keep your mates in awe of you. You quite like poetry and seeing plays – theatre trips are cool – but aren't so keen on novels.

Mostly **d)**s: **The Sociable Reader**. You like reading because it's about people, isn't it? Your attention span isn't very long, so you need a book with a cracking story, about the sort of thing that interests you, maybe a bestseller by a modern writer. You're good on personal response to literature but less certain about how to back up your ideas.

Mostly **e)**s: **The Stroppy Reader**. You like to take the opposite point of view, and have very strong opinions. You probably have a social conscience too, and enjoy a good argument. To interest you, a book's got to have ideas in it, or it needs to be about a social issue. Too much description might get on your nerves.

I reckon I'm a mixture of all five.

Most people are. The kind of reader you are can depend on the mood you're in. Some days you feel more like reading than others. To be good at English Lit, you don't have to be enthusiastic all the time.

I do like reading; otherwise I wouldn't have opted to do literature at GCSE. But reading's not really work, is it?

Depends how you define "work". But the fact you enjoy reading means you're three quarters of the way there.

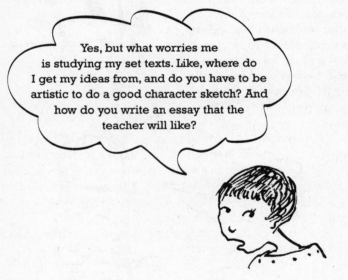

Yes, but what worries me is studying my set texts. Like, where do I get my ideas from, and do you have to be artistic to do a good character sketch? And how do you write an essay that the teacher will like?

Time to get down to brass tacks...

Oh no! Things are getting critical!

First things first. Reading and studying a text are not the same things.

How's that, then?

When you just read you're sitting back and letting the author do most of the work, whether it's to entertain you, to shock you, to make you feel his or her emotions, whatever. When you study a book, you're working with the author to squeeze out all of the meaning in the text, and even suss out exactly how the author manages to put over his or her ideas.

So if you're taking GCSE English Literature, you'll begin to get into the habit of studying texts.

Right. Like we do in lessons.

Could be. Some people do manage to study literature effectively in lessons. For others, it's more like this…

The teacher:

- Reminds the class they should have read the text for last night's homework.
- Reads the text in a thrilling voice.
- Asks a series of ingenious questions about it.
- After a long silence, answers own questions.
- Comments sarcastically on students' lack of attention.
- Digresses to talk about own child's first day at school.
- Warns students there are only six months to the final exams.
- Sets incomprehensible home-work in a rush as the bell goes.

The class:

Listens to first few sentences then begins an intriguing daydream.

Has not read the text but attempts to answer questions to fool teacher.

Oh, no! Things are getting critical!

Tries to follow the lesson but keeps thinking about the chemistry test after lunch.

Has read the text but can't concentrate as missed breakfast and stomach is rumbling.

Read the text, did not understand it, does not understand teacher.

Hopes teacher won't set homework because she is going out tonight.

Has not read the text as rowed with mum last night and they are still not talking.

Just writes down everything teacher says intending to read it later but never does.

Let's face it, studying literature is an artificial thing to do. You end up reading a novel over a whole term, maybe, talking about it in sections, or half a poem one lesson, and the other half five days later. Macbeth is a great play, sure, but not so great when the part of Lady Macbeth is being read by Sharon from 5C in a high-pitched whine and she trips up over all the tricky words.

That's why this section is going to give you sure-fire advice on how to study literature so you can get the most out of the texts in your syllabus.

Studying literature – the five point plan

For each text you study, whether it's poetry, a play, a novel or a short story, there are always FIVE questions you must ask:

1. What is this text about?

2. Why was it written?

3. What were the background or cultural factors that influenced it?

4. How does it achieve its effects or make its points?

5. Do you like it?

Let's have an example.

> **Roses are red,**
> **Violets are blue.**
> **A face like yours**
> **Belongs in the zoo.**

A study of this poem reveals:

1. This verse is about the feeling of contempt the poet has for the receiver of the poem.

2. It was written to insult the receiver.

3. The poet, having visited a safari park the other day, was struck by the resemblance between the orang-utan and his best mate. He also owed his best mate one for splashing his designer trainers with a can of cola.

4. The poem achieves its effect through rhyme, tight rhythm and an unexpected punch-line. The mention of flowers contrast sharply with the suggestion of ugly animal life.

5. No, I don't like it. It's clichéd and I've heard it before. Anyway, it's unfair to animals. Just like zoos are. And furthermore—

...and furthermore -
Strait-jackets
don't even
suit me ....

TOP TIP
It's a good idea never to get too carried away with your own opinions!

Seriously, the method works for all sorts of texts, from the shortest verse to the meatiest novel.

So, HOW do you arrive at the answers to these five questions? Follow this straightforward study plan.

A. If you can, read the text by yourself first.

Why?

It means your opinions about the text are fresh and not too influenced by anyone else.

But what if I don't understand it?

Then you'll need help – and that's NOT a failure on your part. Nobody expects you to understand all your texts straight away – otherwise you wouldn't have Eng Lit lessons, would you? And your literature teachers would be out of jobs. Not only that, the texts you study at GCSE are chosen precisely because they're that little bit more challenging, and need studying if you're going to get the most out of them. So they tend to be more difficult than the kind of book you'd choose by yourself. Remember: If you don't understand all of a text, IT'S NOT YOUR FAULT – it's the text being demanding.

B. Think about the text by talking about it to someone, getting involved in lessons and making notes.

Making notes

Basically, if you're going to study a text seriously, you're going to have to keep a written record of explanations of the tricky bits, and where you get your ideas from. That's why making notes is important.

The main reason I make notes is that I forget all the ideas I have when I read a text for the first time.

In this section we'll look at what makes good notes, and we'll look at an example too.

What are notes helpful for?
- Finding things to say in essays.
- Making texts easier to understand next time you read them.

Where should I keep my notes?
- Ideally, on the text itself. At present every exam board lets you annotate (write brief notes on) your text to help you in the exam. Just make sure your notes are a) legible and b) long enough to be useful, but short enough to satisfy the eagle eye of the invigilator.
- In a notebook. You might also find it useful to have a notebook of your observations, especially for summaries (see page 32). Make sure these notes are eye-catching and make sense to you.

Where do you get your notes from?

- Comments your teacher makes in class.
- Your ideas about the text.
- Your friends' ideas about the text (only don't copy them without thinking them through).

TOP TIP

Be VERY CAREFUL if you're using notes written by someone else – either your teacher, your friend, or notes from a book you've bought to help you with your literature. Other people's ideas are never as clear or useful to you as your own ideas, and examiners have read the commercially produced notes and know when you're using them. If you use the same phrases you find in them, you'll be unmasked as a note-nicker!

What should my notes look like?

- Underline and put squiggles under different important words and phrases.
- Use arrows so you can write brief notes in the margins.
- If you're using a notebook, space out your notes so you can remember their appearance easily. (If you're worried about wasting paper and the shrinking rainforests, just make a donation to Greenpeace after the exam!)

TOP TIP

Don't use too many abbreviations in your notes. You might not remember what you meant by them afterwards. In Shakespeare's play *Macbeth*, you're in for a headache if you shorten both Macbeth and Macduff's names to "Mac"!

What exactly do I put in my notes?

Over to Inspector Holmes, that famous Scotland Yard detective.

"When I visit the scene of a crime – sorry! – literary text, first I make sure I understand exactly what's going on. If there are any details or words that aren't clear, I cross-examine them until I find out exactly what they mean.

Hmm. "Lend me your ears" evidently does not mean the speaker has lost his own, but that he wants the people he's talking to to listen to him for a while!

Friends, Romans, countrymen, lend me your ears.

"Once I've clarified exactly what's happened or is happening, I then start the interrogation. I look for clues to help me work out whodunnit – sorry! – what the writer's really trying to convey.

"Having been a detective for a number of years – excuse me while I just re-fill my pipe – I normally have a checklist in my mind of things to look for – such as fingerprints, stray hairs, dropped possessions, signs of a scuffle. You know, it's an interesting fact, but most criminals leave evidence behind them – it's almost as if part of them wants to get caught. And as it is with criminals, so it is with authors. They leave clues so readers can identify them."

25

In my experience, it's worth looking out for:

- unusual words that imply more than they say.
- interesting words that help create a certain mood or atmosphere.
- similes and metaphors (see page 66).
- comments the author makes about the characters.
- details that form an impression in your mind.

"But most of all, trust your instinct. A good detective has a feel for what really went on at the scene of a crime. A good student of literature has a gut reaction to a text, a hunch, if you like, and then what you have to do is pick up the evidence to support your point of view. Just as I'd never convince a jury my case was watertight without hard evidence, the literature student must be able to give solid proof to back up his or her opinion, and that's where notes come in."

Thank you, Inspector. And now we'll put all this good advice into practice.

Here's the opening of a contemporary novel, *The Sterkarm Handshake*, by Susan Price. In it a group of geologists from the twenty-first century are time-travelling to visit the sixteenth century through a Tube. Let's imagine you were given this to study. You have to decide what the text seems to be about, what mood or atmosphere is being conveyed and you must pick up any clues that will help you get the feel of the book.

First, read this passage by yourself, and if you like, annotate it.

From out of the surrounding hills came a ringing silence that was only deepened by the plodding of the pack-ponies' hooves on the turf and the flirting of their tails against their sides. Above the sky was a clear pale blue, but the breeze was strong.

There were four members of the Geological Survey Team: Malc, Tim, Dave and Caro. They'd left the 21st that morning at eight, coming through the Tube to the 16th, where the plan was to spend four days. None of them had ever been so far from home before, and they often looked back at the Tube. It was their only way back.

It was when they lost sight of the Tube among the folds of the hills, that trouble arrived.

Three horses, with riders, picked their way down the hillside towards them. The horses were all black and thick-set and shaggy, with manes and tails hanging almost to the ground. The riders' helmets had been blackened with soot and grease, to keep them from rust, or covered with sheepskin so they looked like hats. Their other clothes were all buffs and browns, blending into the buffs, browns and greens all around them. Their long leather riding boots rose over the knee. On they came with a clumping of hooves and a jangling of harness, carrying eight-foot-long lances with ease...

The first to dismount, his lance still in his hand, was probably the eldest. He was bearded, but no older than about twenty. He went straight up to Malc and began to pull the back-pack from his shoulders.

"I thought they'd agreed not to rob us any more," Caro said, taking off her own back-pack as the other dismounted rider came towards her.

"Just don't annoy them," Malc said.

As Dave and Tim shrugged out of their back-packs, one of the bearded footmen called out something – in a speech that sounded like coughing and snarling. His companions all laughed.

The geologists looked anxiously at each other. They didn't understand the joke, and were afraid of

27

how far it might be taken.

The second dismounted rider suddenly caught Tim's hand and pulled his arm out straight. For a moment Tim looked into an almost beardless and strikingly pretty face – and then the young man was dragging at his wrist-watch, pulling the expandable bracelet off over his hand. He stared Tim in the face for a moment, and then snatched off the geologist's spectacles before moving on to Dave and grabbing at his hands too...

Malc caught sight of Caro's face, set in a grimace of fright. The other two looked much the same, and he supposed that his own face also reflected his painful uncertainty and fear.

Good, isn't it? Now look at this annotated version, and compare it with yours.

From out of the surrounding hills came a

how can a silence 'ring'? Interesting!

ringing silence that was only deepened by the

ponies kept for carrying things

plodding of the pack-ponies' hooves on the turf and

the flirting of their tails against their sides. Above the sky was a clear pale blue, but the breeze was strong.

silence & emptiness makes it sound remote

There were four members of the Geological Survey Team: Malc, Tim, Dave and Caro. They'd left the 21st that morning at eight, coming through the

centuries

Tube to the <u>16th</u>, where the plan was to spend four

days. None of them had ever been so far from home before, and they often looked back at the <u>Tube</u>. It was their only way back.

↑ *builds up tension.*
  What if they can't get back?   *time travelling*
                                     Tube

It was when they lost sight of the Tube among the folds of the hills, that trouble arrived. ←

builds up even more tension! We expect trouble)

Three horses, with riders, picked their way down the hillside towards them. The horses were all <u>black</u>

and thick-set and <u>shaggy</u>, with manes and tails

sounds sinister

<u>hanging almost to the ground. The riders' helmets had been blackened with soot</u> and

interesting historical detail

grease, to keep them from rust, or covered with sheepskin so they looked like hats. Their other

a dull yellow colour

clothes were all <u>buffs</u> and browns, blending into the

buffs, browns and greens all around them. Their long leather riding boots rose over the knee. On they came with a <u>clumping</u> of hooves and a

sound words makes writing vivid

jangling of harness, carrying eight-foot-long lances

with ease... *(scary!)*

The first to dismount, his lance still in his hand, was probably the eldest. He was bearded, but no older than about twenty. He went straight up to Malc and began to pull the back-pack from his shoulders.

"I thought they'd agreed not to rob us any more," Caro said, taking off her own back-pack as

she's obviously too scared to put up a fight

the other dismounted rider came towards her. "Just don't annoy them," Malc said. *so is he*

As Dave and Tim shrugged out of their

good word helps us see the movement

back-packs, one of the bearded footmen called out something – in a speech that sounded like coughing and snarling. His companions all laughed.

sinister verbs

The geologists looked anxiously at each other. They didn't understand the joke, and were afraid of how far it might be taken.

The second dismounted rider suddenly caught Tim's hand and pulled his arm out straight. For a moment Tim looked into an almost beardless and strikingly pretty face – and then the young man

unexpected – is this going to be important later?

was dragging at his wrist-watch, pulling the expandable bracelet off over his hand. He stared Tim in the face for a moment, and then snatched off the geologist's spectacles before moving on to Dave and grabbing at his hands too...

Malc caught sight of Caro's face, set in a grimace of fright. The other two looked much the

vivid description

same, and he supposed that his own face also reflected his painful uncertainty and fear.

Malc's feelings stated

4 chars – Malc, Tim, Dave, Caro. 3 horsemen. A sinister, arresting opening – will the geologists get away?

Don't worry if the points you made were different – the aim of this exercise is just to get into the habit of making notes, and laying them out properly. Chapter two on page 49 will help you decide exactly what to put in your notes.

> OK. I can see that it's a good idea to annotate texts, especially since I'm allowed to take annotated texts into the exam. But do I have to bother with any other sort of notes?

If you mean business, I think you do. Every literature student will end up writing essays about their texts, normally with the text in front of them. So you don't have to memorize them word for word, but you DO have to know them pretty well so you can plan an essay quickly. Notes can help you get to know your text, and there are three particular kinds of notes that help you do that:

1. Summaries
2. Grids
3. Character Sketches

Summaries

When you're studying a longer text such as a play or novel, it really will pay to keep a brief summary of the storyline.

For a **play**, make a subheading for each scene, list the characters appearing in it, and say in a sentence or two what happens. You might even add a key quotation or two.

For example:

> **Macbeth And Juliet**
> **Act One: Scene One**
> **Macbeth**
> **Juliet**
> **The Nurse**
> **The Three Witches**

Juliet enters on to a windswept heath and dishes the goss with the three witches. Macbeth enters and tells Juliet he has fallen in love with the Nurse. The Nurse enters and the witches curse her. Long soliloquy by Juliet in which she says she's going to emigrate to Venice and disguise herself as a man.
"Fair is foul and foul is fair"

For a **novel**, make your summary chapter by chapter, sub-dividing chapters if they seem very long to you. It's not so important to list characters – just get the main points of the plot.

For example:

Of Mice And Mockingbirds
Chapter 3

Lenny knocks on the Radley front door and Boo answers. Boo invites Lenny in for tea and he asks if there are any rabbits. Boo says he's not allowed pets but suggests they play cutting the newspaper into strips. They do this until Mr Nathan Radley comes home from work.

Poetry grids

If you're studying a collection of poetry, obviously a summary isn't much use to you. A poem doesn't always have a story – it could be simply a description or some thoughts. You need to have a different method for keeping a record of what you study. A poetry grid is ideal.

Collections of poetry at GCSE are often about one theme – the seasons, animals, war, etc. Or the collection could be by just one poet. Inevitably the poems will have some things in common. A poetry grid will help you see this more clearly.

To show you how it works, look at the following poems:

Cat

Golden eyes that glint dangerously
Paws with sheathed sharp talons
Pause with sheathed sharp talons
And pounce
The screaming death-throes of the back-broken
    mouse rend the sky.

Puss

I stroke her soft and silken fur
I baby-talk; she gives a purr
And rubs herself against my chest
I tell her that I love her best
She treads my lap with half-closed eyes
Settles down and on me lies.

Patrol

Out through the cat flap I appear
And sidle by the wall
I am not very tall
I prick up each pointed ear
And slowly leap on to the fence
Once up, I sniff the air

Then walk along with care
On red alert is every sense
My whiskers twitch and quiver
I dive back to the ground
A butterfly I've found
Then I trot down to the river.

Fight

As she sees him her teeth bare
In a ferocious snarl
Her inner tiger stands revealed.
Her opponent, tabby, scraggy, back arched, tail a
    question-mark of anxiety, doubt, defensiveness
She advances, slinking black evil
Her paw shoots out and the tabby howls, hides, spits
She leaps on him biting, scratching, the old, black
    harridan
She-witch, murderess, black death.

The litter

Four tiny bodies, writhing close to each other
For comfort, for warmth, in fierce competition for
    their mother's teats
They wriggle, push and shove
The mother: is it love
She feels for these worm-like, warm, white wanderers
With their eyes tight shut, their instincts alert, sniffing
    for the milk
One starts in bliss to suck
The others gently tuck
Themselves into the folds of the purring, whirring
    mother cat.

	About?	Viewpoint it's written from	Does it rhyme?	Is it free verse?	Does it use lists for description	Cats shown as violent?	Cats shown as gentle?	A typical quotation
Cat	A cat killing a mouse	Detached observer	No	Yes	No	Yes	No	"sheathed sharp talons"
Puss	A cat settling down on a lap	First person – the owner	Yes (a,a,b,b,c,c)	No	No	No	Yes	"soft + silken fur"
Patrol	A cat patrolling its territory	First person – the cat	Yes (a,b,b,a,c, d,d,c etc)	No	No	No	Slightly	"I prick up each pointed ear"
Fight	A cat fight	Detached observer	No	Yes	Yes	Yes	No	"She-witch, murderess, black death"
The litter	A litter of new-born kittens	Detached observer	Some Rhyme	Yes	Yes	Slightly	Slightly	"Worm-like, warm white wanderers"

The five poems all describe cats, but initially that seems to be where the similarity ends. A poetry grid helps you see clearly what features the poems might have in common.

Down one side you print the title of the poems, and along the top you decide what heading to give the columns, depending on the kind of poems you're studying. Here the grid looks at style (rhyme, free verse, the habit of the poet of using lists) and content and attitude to cats (cats as violent, cats as gentle). Putting your observations in a table like this is very useful when it comes to planning poetry essays.

Character sketches

Literature is more fun to study than any other GCSE because it's about people, what they're like, what they do and what makes them tick. Just like you enjoy sitting around talking about your mates, or wondering how on earth she could go out with him (you know who I mean!), it's interesting sizing up characters in a text. And it's what the author wants you to do. That's why you're going to need to make notes on characters – in other words, compose a character sketch.

But first, some thoughts on how we decide on character.

Say someone new is joining your class or club or neighbourhood. You get to meet them. All the time you're busy working out what you think of them, whether you like them or not. How do you do this? You interpret signals. Here are some of them:

What's the expression on their face like?
What are they wearing?
What's their hair like?
How do they speak?
What are their bike, watch, trainers like?
What are their interests?
Where do they hang out?
What do they say to you?

How do they behave?
Do they like the same people you like?
What do other people think of them?

Suppose a bloke…
- Grins in a friendly way
- Wears Hilfiger jeans and sweatshirt
- Has short, fashionable hair
- Speaks your language and shares your sense of humour
- Has expensive gear – and is that Rolex genuine?
- Likes skiing, snowboarding, mountain biking, clubbing
- Has already been seen in all the cool places
- Is friendly and eager to please, agreeing with what you say
- Seems popular with your mates

Have you reached any conclusions? He's obviously rich, but that hasn't gone to his head. You feel you'd like him if you got to know him as he's keen to get on with people, and he's on your wavelength. The signs are that he'd make a good mate (and he'd be cool to be seen with!). That's the character analysis based on the evidence we've collected. Let's try it again. Imagine a girl who…

- Pouts, half-smiles, looks at people, then looks away
- Is wearing a short skirt, a tiny vest top, high platforms and shiny lipstick
- Spends ages doing her hair, copying a style from this month's teen mag
- Has a voice that is low and sexy when she talks to boys but high and strident when she's with other girls

- Has three excellent mates and they hang around all the time
- Likes the latest boy band and parties and boys
- Never misses a party or club night
- Is only interested in finding out who you know
- Thinks all of your friends are nerds

She's a typical socialite (to put it mildly), into having a good time and looking her very best. A bit of a flirt too? I think so. We deduced all that just from details about her appearance, manners and behaviour.

In literature, you work out character in exactly the same way. You might not get as much information as that, but you might get even more – for example, the writer might tell you what to think.

Let's move straight on to the hard stuff. In the following extract from Jane Austen's novel *Pride and Prejudice*, we are meeting the two heroes, Bingley and Darcy, for the first time, and we have to make up our minds about them…

Mr Bingley was good-looking and gentleman-like; he had a pleasant countenance, and easy, unaffected manners. His sisters were fine women, with an air of decided fashion. His brother-in-law, Mr Hurst, merely looked the gentleman; but his friend, Mr Darcy soon drew the attention of the room by his fine, tall person, handsome features, noble mien, and the report, which was in general circulation within five minutes after his entrance, of his having ten thousand a year. The gentlemen pronounced him to be a fine figure of a man, the ladies declared he was much handsomer than Mr Bingley, and he was looked at with great admiration for about half the evening, till his manners gave a disgust which turned the tide of his popularity: for he was discovered to be proud, to be above his company, and above being pleased; and not all his large estate in Derbyshire could then save him from having a most forbidding, disagreeable countenance, and being unworthy to be compared with his friend.

Mr Bingley had soon made himself acquainted with all the principal people in the room: he was lively and unreserved, danced every dance, was angry that the ball closed so early, and talked of giving one himself at Netherfield. Such amiable qualities must speak for themselves. What a contrast between him and his friend! Mr Darcy danced only once with Mrs Hurst, and once with Miss Bingley, declined being introduced to any other lady, and spent the rest of the evening in walking about the room, speaking occasionally to one of his own party. His character was decided. He was the proudest, most disagreeable man in the world, and everybody hoped that he would never come there again.

What do we learn about Bingley?

He's good-looking, has a pleasant countenance (nice face), and easy, unaffected manners (polite but not showy about it). So he comes across as likeable through the way he speaks, the expression on his face and his general behaviour.

His sisters are "fine women" meaning smart and fashionable, so he is probably fairly smart and fashionable too – we tend to judge someone from the company they keep.

Bingley introduces himself to all the movers and shakers at the ball, dances all evening, and evidently likes dancing – he wants to give a ball of his own at his place (Netherfield). So we know he's friendly through his actions, and that his interests include socializing and dancing. Everybody at the ball liked him. When Jane Austen says "Such amiable [likeable] qualities must speak for themselves" she is voicing the view of the people at the ball. We don't actually know what the writer thinks of him. Writers can be awkward customers occasionally and hold back from giving us their true opinions.

So, we can conclude Bingley is a nice bloke – friendly, outgoing, sociable, good-looking, a catch (if you're female). What's more, we have all the evidence to prove it!

And what about Darcy?

We find out he's tall, handsome and has a "noble mien" (mien means look or manner). Also, he's rich. As soon as the people at the ball find out he's rich they like him more than ever, but when they discover he's also proud and "above being pleased" – we'd say snobby – they go right off him. How do they know he's proud? Through his actions – he only dances with the ladies he came with and doesn't talk to anyone else. So, we can work out his initial character from his appearance, the opinions of other people, the contrast with Bingley, and his actions – he's rich, classy, good-looking but possibly a snob. The really attentive reader, however, will question whether he's a snob, because his actions (staying with his own friends) could be those of a shy person. Rich people can be shy too.

If you were beginning to build up character sketches of Bingley and Darcy, it would be useful for you to put the points you've discovered about them, together with the evidence, in columns like this:

POINT	EVIDENCE
Bingley is likeable.	"Pleasant countenance, and easy, unaffected manners". Also everyone at the ball likes him.
He seems fashionable.	His sisters are fashionable – we judge him by them.
He's friendly.	He likes socialising, dancing, he introduces himself to everyone at the ball.

Evidence in character sketches can EITHER be quotations (remember to put quotation marks around them if they're the writer's own words) OR things the characters do summed up. Think of quotations as HARD evidence, and make sure you always include some in a character sketch.

If we carry this method on for Darcy, what evidence would you put down to prove the following points?

1. He's rich.

2. People admire him to begin with.

3. He's proud (or possibly shy).

Answers on page 199.

Once you've made notes on a character in this way, imagine how straightforward it would be to write an essay all about them... (See chapter four on page 132.)

One last opportunity for you to prove to yourself you can work out character in this way. Below is an extract from Harper Lee's novel *To Kill A Mockingbird*. Here the character Dill (a young boy) is introduced for the first time. What impressions do you form of him? How did you form those impressions?

Read the passage, then record your findings in two columns: Point and Evidence. Good luck!

> **Early one morning as we were beginning our day's play in the back yard, Jem and I heard something next door in Miss Rachel Haverford's collard patch. We went to the wire fence to see if there was a puppy – Miss Rachel's rat terrier was expecting – instead we found someone sitting looking at us. Sitting down, he wasn't much higher than the collards. We stared at him until he spoke:**
> **"Hey."**

"Hey yourself," said Jem pleasantly.

"I'm Charles Baker Harris," he said. "I can read."

"So what?" I said.

"I just thought you'd like to know I can read. You got anything needs readin' I can do it..."

"How old are you," asked Jem, "four-and-a-half?"

"Goin' on seven."

"Shoot no wonder then," said Jem, jerking his thumb at me. "Scout yonder's been readin' ever since she was born, and she ain't even started to school yet. You look right puny for goin' on seven."

"I'm little but I'm old," he said.

Jem brushed his hair back to get a better look. "Why don't you come over, Charles Baker Harris?" he said. "Lord, what a name."

"'S not any funnier'n yours. Aunt Rachel says your name's Jeremy Atticus Finch."

Jem scowled. "I'm big enough to fit mine," he said. "Your name's longer'n you are. Bet it's a foot longer."

"Folks call me Dill," said Dill, struggling under the fence.

CLUE!

We learn about Dill's character mainly through what he says and his appearance.

Possible answer on page 199.

Any other points you thought of – provided you've got evidence – are almost certainly correct. The skill of constructing a good character sketch is to provide the *evidence*.

43

So it doesn't matter what you say as long as you've got the evidence? I could say that because the three witches always hang round together they must be best friends, which proves they're all nice people and so it must have been Macbeth who tempted them and the only reason they boil something up in the cauldron is that they all want to be TV chefs?

Well, at least you've shown you have a good imagination. Also, you've made an important point.

I have?

Definitely. When we interpret a text (work out what the writer is trying to say) we're free to have our own opinions UP TO A POINT. In literature, nothing is ever black and white; part of the fun of reading is deciding what you think about a certain poem or novel or play. But obviously there are limits, as you've just shown by your theory about the three witches. Sometimes it's tricky to see what these limits are.

People who do well at Eng Lit are most often those people who get a feel for what they can and what they can't say about a certain text. Here are some guidelines for you.

You're probably right if you...
- Have sensible evidence to back yourself up.
- Can find evidence from more than one part of the text.
- Can't find any contradictory evidence.
- Are thinking logically and getting seriously involved with the text.

You're probably wrong if you...
- Are going outside the text to make your point (speculating about what could have happened to the characters before or after the text takes place).
- Are providing no evidence.
- Are being too influenced by your own situation or agenda ("I like this poem because the person who wrote it has the same first name as me" or "I don't like this poem because it's about snakes and I'm frightened of snakes" or "I don't like the typeface the printer uses for this poem").
- Are saying or writing the first thing you think without testing your theory.

Now practise your own critical skills on the following poem, "Afternoons", by Philip Larkin.

Philip Larkin was born in 1922 and died in 1985. He was British and liked writing poetry about everyday things. He was also a librarian, loved jazz and was offered the post of Poet Laureate, but declined.

First read the poem and think about Larkin's attitude to the young mothers he is describing. Then read the three interpretations below. Two of them are right even though they take a different approach. One of them is totally wrong. Can you work out which is which?

Afternoons
Summer is fading:
The leaves fall in ones and twos
From trees bordering
The new recreation ground.
In the hollows of afternoons
Young mothers assemble
At swing and sandpit
Setting free their children.

Behind them, at intervals,
Stand husbands in skilled trades,
An estateful of washing,
And the albums, lettered
Our Wedding, lying
Near the television:
Before them, the wind
Is ruining their courting-places

That are still courting-places
(But the lovers are all in school),
And their children, so intent on
Finding more unripe acorns,
Expect to be taken home.

46

Their beauty has thickened.
Something is pushing them
To the side of their own lives.

a) Larkin feels sorry for the young mothers he is describing. There is a sad atmosphere in the first stanza ("summer is fading", the afternoons are described as having "hollows", as if they are empty). All their lives consist of is loads of washing and looking after children, and "the wind/Is ruining their courting-places", meaning the places where they flirted with their husbands are disappearing. Then Larkin says those places are being used by kids at school, which makes us feel the young mothers are getting older. They just don't have lives of their own anymore, nor anything to look forward to. Just as summer changes into autumn so these mothers are changing.

b) Larkin thinks the young mothers are worse than the people who vandalize parks. They "set free" their children there and the leaves falling sounds like litter being dropped. I hate it when people drop litter. Once I tripped on a banana skin and broke my leg and had to go to hospital. You can tell the women are messy because they leave their wedding albums out by the television sets. In our house my mum keeps hers in the cupboard in the front room. Probably these young mothers had to get married and didn't really love their husbands, so they're taking it out on their children and go around vandalizing the park. They scatter "unripe acorns" everywhere.

c) Even though it might sound like Larkin feels sorry for these mothers, there are touches in the poem that make me wonder if that's right. First of all, he writes about them as if they're a big, nameless group. They just "assemble" in the park. They sound as if they don't have minds of their own. When he says they "set free" their children it gives the impression the children are imprisoned at home, and the mothers might be the jailers. The fact the wedding albums are left near the television make the mothers seem silly and sentimental, always looking back to the day of their wedding, and not living in the real world of today. He writes "Their beauty has thickened," which makes them appear unattractive.

What conclusions did you reach?

a) and c) are both right. In fact, you could say that Larkin's true feelings about the young mothers he describes are mixed, and they are the more interesting for that. b) is completely off his trolley. He speculates, talks about himself and supplies no hard evidence even though he drops in the occasional quotation.

Now you know *how to study a text*, you're ready to move on to *what to look for* in a text…

How does that writer do it?

NEWS OF THE SUN

ENG LIT GCSE EXAMINER TRAPPED INTO GIVING AWAY TOP SECRETS

Yesterday, in a hotel in an undisclosed location, a chief examiner confessed why it is that some Eng Lit candidates do better than others.

Our intrepid reporter, Charlotte Austen, lured him to the hotel with promises of a suite of rooms lined wall to wall with volumes of poetry, and promised him non-stop reading of nineteenth-century novels in return for these steamy revelations. The examiner cracked immediately.

"We would like to give all candidates top grades. But

we don't," he said, in between reciting Shakespearian soliloquies. "To be absolutely honest with you, we tend to see candidates in three groups. The bottom group can only just about tell the story of the texts they've read, or sometimes can't even do that. The middle group can say what the text is about and perhaps make points about characters and answer a question. But the top group – no – I can't tell you any more – it's more than my job's worth!"

Our reporter then seduced him with a line of iambic pentameter.

"All right. The top group actually pay attention to HOW a text is written. They look at the writer's methods. They look at the devices the writer uses and say how those devices affect the text. They know the tools of the trade. They're alert to a writer's techniques. They're wonderful. If I could meet one, I'd clone them. Have you got any caesuras on you?"

It's true. If you seriously want to get top marks at Eng Lit GCSE you've got to get the lowdown on writers' techniques. This section is a cheat's guide to the most common tools of their trade. When you've read and digested this, you'll never be lost for things to say in an essay again.

As an introduction, just consider the following few statements, all of which are saying more or less the same thing. But just look at the differences between them.

Darling, be an absolute treasure and put on the kettle.

You can jolly well get off your backside and make me a cuppa.

Make me a cup of tea, if you please.

A cup of tea, two sugars and go easy on the milk.

Hey baby, get it together with the kettle and the hot water.

Oy! You! Tea!

As you can see, *how* you say something affects the meaning very much. Some of the above requests for a cup of tea were downright rude, others were cajoling or funny. Matters like the choice of words, the order of words and even the rhythm, affect meaning. That's why looking at writers' techniques is so important.

Since we like to make things simple for you, we're going to divide writers' favourite techniques into three easy-to-handle groups:

- **WordsWorth** – takes a look at the words writers use
- **It's ... like ... er ...** – examines how writers use comparisons
- **Designer Lit** – gives the lowdown on writers' structure and tone

WordsWorth

This group includes a look at diction, alliteration, word order and rhythm.

Read on – all will be revealed...

1. Diction

All diction means is *choice of words*. To help you remember that, think of a dictionary, which offers you a very large choice of words. Writers know they can achieve some very interesting effects by the words they use.

A good way to look at it is by comparing writers to painters. Just as painters use paints in different colours, shades and textures, writers use words.

It's common sense, I know, but it's easy when you're studying literature to get sidetracked by the difficult aspects of the subject and not see the obvious.

So always remember to consider the choice of words the writer makes – his or her diction.

When looking at diction, there are *two* things to look for. We'll consider each separately.

a) Word associations

Most words tend to remind you of other words or ideas. No word exists in a vacuum. You can prove this by the Name Game.

Here is a list of eight names. Read them through fairly quickly.

Steve	**Ahmed**	**Camille**	**Sebastian**
Donna	**Lisa**	**Mark**	**Rachel**

I bet you've already formed impressions of what the owners of those names are like. Your impressions have been formed by the people that you know who have those names. If you know someone called Mark or Rachel, the names made you think of them. Maybe you thought of Sebastian as someone a bit more posh than the others. That could be an association you have with that name.

Words are like names. When we read them, we have associations that are present in our minds. Look at the diagram below:

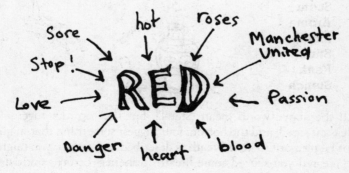

The word "red" has associations with all the words around it. These are associations that most of us are familiar with. For example, everyone stops at a red traffic light (or ought to).

When you're looking closely at a text and you want to think about diction, ask yourself if the word you're considering has any common associations.

b) Positive or negative?

Relax – this book has not suddenly become a science text book. You're safe. Instead you're going to be asked to think about the way words can be either happy or sad, or how they can convey either approval or disapproval.

The English language is rich in words that mean nearly the same as other words. So writers are spoilt for choice when it comes to words. The exact word a writer picks matters. It really matters. Just as you don't go shopping for clothes and pick any old jeans or top – they have to look absolutely right for you to cough up the dosh – so a writer doesn't just pick any old words. They're fussy.

To see how a writer can voice approval or disapproval, we need to look at a word chain.

Fragrance
Perfume
Scent
Aroma
Smell
Stink
Reek
Stench

All the above words mean "smell", but the top four suggest a pleasant smell, and the bottom four suggest something that might not be pleasant. If your breath is described as fragrant, you might be pleased you sucked some breath fresheners before your date. But look what Shakespeare says in one poem about the woman he likes:

> And in some perfumes is there more delight
> Than in the breath that from my mistress reeks.

"Reeks" is hardly a flattering description of someone's breath. In fact, when you read the whole poem this quotation is taken from, you see that Shakespeare is actually complimenting his mistress in a roundabout way, despite the apparent insult.

> My mistress' eyes are nothing like the sun;
> Coral is far more red than her lips' red;
> If snow be white, why then her breasts are dun;
> If hairs be wires, black wires grow on her head.
> I have seen roses damask'd, red and white,
> But no such roses see I in her cheeks;
> And in some perfumes is there more delight
> Than in the breath that from my mistress reeks.
> I love to hear her speak, yet well I know
> That music hath a far more pleasing sound;
> I grant I never saw a goddess go –
> My mistress when she walks treads on the ground.
> And yet, by heaven, I think my love as rare
> As any she belied with false compare.

Now try a word chain yourself. Put the following six words in order from the most positive to the most negative.

lanky, willowy, bony, skeletal, slender, slim

Answers on page 199.

When a writer uses positive words, he or she is conveying some approval or liking of what is being described; similarly, negative words show disapproval. If you can work out accurately the writer's feelings about the subject of their writing, then you're well on the way to becoming a GCSE success.

Test yourself. Here's a shortened description by Charles Dickens of a character who ... but *you* decide. How does Dickens let us know how he feels about the character he has created? Look at the key words he uses and begin by asking yourself whether they're positive or negative.

> **He had but one eye, and the popular prejudice runs in favour of two. The blank side of his face was much wrinkled, and puckered up, which gave him a very sinister appearance, especially when he smiled, at which times his expression bordered closely on the villainous. His hair was very flat and shiny, save at the ends, where it was brushed stiffly up from a low, protruding forehead, which assorted well with his harsh voice and coarse manner.**

Certainly a man we'll love to hate! The diction that gives the game away includes "wrinkled", "puckered up", "sinister", "villainous", "harsh" and "coarse". This is a portrait of the bullying schoolmaster Mr Squeers from *Nicholas Nickleby*.

Try practising your new skill of noticing diction whenever you read – the more you do it, the easier it gets.

TOP TIP

The more words you know, the easier it is to notice what a writer is doing with diction, so **increase your own vocabulary**.

- Read as much as possible.
- Look up new and unfamiliar words in a dictionary or ask someone who knows what a new word means.
- Try to use new words shortly after meeting them so you remember what they mean.
- Buy books of word puzzles or crosswords and do those for fun.
- Watch word games on TV.
- Stop your English teacher whenever he or she uses a word you don't know, and ask what the word means. And remember – never be ashamed of admitting you don't know what a word means. It's much more embarrassing to pretend you do know, and then get caught out...

Diction is one of the main tools used to convey *mood and atmosphere*. Just look at the opening of Charlotte Bronte's *Jane Eyre*:

> There was no possibility of taking a walk that day.
>
> We had been wandering, indeed, in the leafless shrubbery an hour in the morning; but since dinner (Mrs Reed, when there was no company, dined early) the cold winter wind had brought with it clouds so sombre, and a rain so penetrating, that further outdoor exercise was out of the question.
>
> I was glad of it: I never liked long walks, especially on chilly afternoons; dreadful to me was the coming home in the raw twilight, with nipped fingers and toes...

With diction such as "leafless", "cold", "winter", "clouds", "sombre", "rain", "chilly", "dreadful", "raw" and "nipped" there can be little question of the mood the writer wants to establish – utterly bleak and depressing. And establishing a mood like this makes us feel sorry for the speaker, in this case the heroine Jane Eyre.

Basically, diction is as important to literature as petrol is to a car!

2. Alliteration

Alliteration occurs when a writer deliberately makes words close to each other begin with the same letter or sound.

For example:

The buffalo bellowed bravely. (b)
Shyly she showed me the champagne. (sh)
The leaves of the willow whispered winningly. (w)

Alliteration is one of the easiest writer's devices to spot. You'll tend to find it more in poetry than in prose.

> In Anglo-Saxon times, no English poetry rhymed. Instead it was written in half-lines with a gap in between, and on each side of the gap, words were linked by the same initial letter ... alliteration! Yes – alliteration is one of the earliest poetic devices known to mankind!

Shakespeare used alliteration too, but here he's poking fun at the way it can be over-used. This is Pyramus going over the top with it in *A Midsummer Night's Dream*.

58

...with blade, with bloody blameful blade,
He bravely broach'd his boiling bloody breast;
And Thisby, tarrying in mulberry shade,
His dagger drew, and died.

Yes, alliteration is easy to spot, but not so easy to comment on.
Avoid making the sort of mistakes that make the examiner blush
by following this failproof list of dos and don'ts.

When commenting on alliteration:

DO

- Say the use of alliteration intensifies the effect of the line or words, or shows how closely they are connected.
- Notice that some letters can have a specific effect, for example:
  B   has an explosive sound
  D   is a hard sound
  L   has a liquid sound
  M   can have a humming effect
  S   can have a hissing effect

DON'T

- Claim silly things for other letters, e.g. "the 'p' alliteration makes me think of horses".
- Spend too long commenting on alliteration – it's only a minor literary device.
- Say it makes the line *flow* – only rivers and streams flow, not lines of poetry.

In fact, alliteration is so easy to spot you'll find it's equally easy to play with it yourself. If you fancy you can practise your poetic prowess and your virtuosity at varying your vocabulary. You could write a short non-rhyming poem with as many words as possible beginning with the same letter (e.g. Pretty prancing poppies purpled the pasture...) or how about an alliterative story (e.g.

Andrea Applethwaite ambled aimlessly by the Bull and Bush and brushed past David Daneman who was dashing directly to the dentist…).

3. Word order

Imagine this. You're going to the party of the year. You want to make a serious impression. You have the right gear, your hair looks great, and all you have to worry about is the right time to arrive. You want to stand out from the crowd. You want to be noticed. The party starts at 9 p.m. When do you arrive?

a) 8.50, and you position yourself just where you can be seen to your best advantage by everyone coming in.
b) 9.30, along with everyone else.
c) 10.30, and make a dramatic entrance.

Well, **b)** is definitely the wrong response. You'll be lost in the crowd. **a)** or **c)** will do nicely. Either way, you're sure to be seen.

So it is with a writer's sentences. They're cunningly ordered so that the most important words get the best position. And the best position is generally right at the beginning or right at the end.

The owl hooted, and we knew that night had fallen.

Into the ring, accompanied by a chorus of catcalls and jeers, stepped the 22-stone Giant Beanbag.

In the first sentence, the emphasis is thrown on the hooting of the owl. In the second, there's a dramatic build-up to the climax of the wrestler entering the ring. See how much less effective these sentences are with another word order.

We knew that night had fallen because the owl hooted.

Boring.

Giant Beanbag, who weighs 22 stone, stepped into the ring accompanied by a chorus of catcalls and jeers.

Or even...

A chorus of catcalls and jeers accompanied Giant Beanbag, who weighed 22 stone, as he stepped into the ring.

Neither of these versions have the element of suspense that the first version has.

Look at this opening to a short story by Graham Greene.

It was on the eve of August Bank Holiday that the latest recruit became the leader of the Wormsley Common Gang.

The sentence begins in a matter-of-fact way, giving the date, but then goes on to relate the main fact – there's a new leader in the Wormsley Common Gang. The mention of the gang, left till the end, is the interesting bit. We are tempted to read on and find out what the gang is, and who the leader is. Word order plays an important part in that.

Now look at these few lines from a poem by Robert Browning, a Victorian, describing a murder. You can just feel the suspense building up, and look where Browning places the murder in his sentence.

I found
A thing to do, and all her hair
In one long yellow string I wound
Three times her little throat around,
And strangled her.

> OK. I can see that. So are you trying to say that when a writer sits down to write they consciously think about word order? Because I don't when I write, otherwise I'd never have time to finish anything.

No, I'm not. None of these writers' techniques is necessarily a conscious process. Writers often write by instinct – images and word order occur to them and they have a feeling they're right. The words feel right and sound right. It's like a painter working on a canvas, who steps back, looks at his or her creation, and thinks, "Yes! That's it!" Or like a songwriter trying out a few chords and liking the combination.

4. Rough guide to rhythm
We all know what rhythm is, but few of us can either spell it or define it. Learn to spell it by reciting R-H-Y-T-H-M, and define it by saying that it means a regular, measurable beat. In poetry or sometimes prose it's the beat that words make. Musicians use rhythm too, of course, so beat out a rhythm with your hand and get into the swing of this section.

No, seriously, beat out a rhythm. Now.

Some of the beats you made were shorter and quicker than others. Beat out your rhythm again and listen.

It's the same in poetry. Some sounds are shorter than others. In poetry, the sound unit we use is not a word, but a *syllable* – a syllable always contains one vowel sound and usually consonants before or after.

> **Big – one syllable**
> **Bigger – two syllables**
> **Enormous – three syllables**
> **Overwhelming – four syllables**

Some syllables are LONG (take a longer time to say) and some are SHORT (take a shorter time to say). The bad news is, it's almost impossible to detect how much longer one syllable takes to say than another. Try it; listen to your mates speak – they probably just gabble. The good news is, you can use this failproof method to work out if a syllable is short or long.

Long syllables
Either have a vowel which sound likes the name of the letter:
A (ay), E (ee), I (eye) O (oh) U (you)
Or have a double vowel (ee, oo)
Or sound like *hour, or, air, ear, ire, ah.*

Short syllables
Have vowels which sound like the way we pronounce them in the alphabet.

a (as in cat)	o (as in dog)
e (as in egg)	u (as in cup)
i (as in fish)	

Say if the following syllables are short or long:

1. Tip **2.** Laugh **3.** Map **4.** Wow! **5.** Nut **6.** Chest

Answers on page 199.

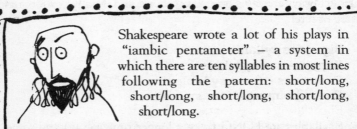

Shakespeare wrote a lot of his plays in "iambic pentameter" – a system in which there are ten syllables in most lines following the pattern: short/long, short/long, short/long, short/long, short/long.

Unless you're hell-bent on travelling back in a time capsule to the Elizabethan Age you won't need to write in iambic pentameter, or comment on it. At GCSE, however, you should try to be able to work out if the rhythm of a piece of writing is fast or slow, by looking at the syllable length.

Sometimes a syllable has a short vowel sound but several consonants surround it, which makes it take longer to say.

Try saying **stretch**
Or **bridge**
Or **prompt**

A few of these can slow a line down just as much as too many long vowels. Think of these sort of consonant-full syllables as being like a short person with platforms and a tall hat.

Generally, SLOW rhythms have a few long syllables. ("The cow mooed slowly.") FAST rhythms have quite a few short syllables. ("Let us run to the hut.")

SLOW rhythm is often used when the mood of a text is sad, or the writer wishes to create a weary atmosphere.

FAST rhythm can be used to create a happier mood, or a mood of tense anxiety and suspense. For example...

> **Humpty Dumpty sat on a wall**
> **Humpty Dumpty had a great fall...**
>
> **The rhythm here is:**
> **Short long, short long, short short short long.**
> **Short long, short long, short short long long.**
> **The long sounds at the end of the second line**
> **emphasize the grave nature of Humpty's descent.**

Seriously, we can use this technique of looking at rhythm whenever we consider a poem.

> **Yes, I remember Adlestrop –**
> **The name, because one afternoon**
> **Of heat the express-train drew up there**
> **Unwontedly. It was late June.**

(Unwontedly means unusually. This is the beginning of a descriptive poem about an unscheduled train halt in the English countryside.)

At the beginning of this poem there are quite a few short syllables ("remember Adle"), giving a brisk opening. Then the verse slows down with some long syllables ("one afternoon/Of heat") which is appropriate as the poet is describing the sort of warmth that makes you drowsy, and the fact the train had stopped! The same effect occurs at the end of the verse "It was late June." Those two final long syllables carry on the sleepy effect.

It's enough just to comment briefly on rhythm – you don't want to give a blow-by-blow analysis of every line. That would get sooo boring. Just pick out one or two moments when the rhythm seems to contribute something to the verse. Look particularly for matching content and rhythm – a sad occasion being described with long syllables, say.

And don't worry if you can't quite get your head round rhythm. It's one of the trickier aspects of lit crit and you should only attempt to comment on it if you feel confident. (But after reading this section you can feel that confidence beginning to course through your veins!)

What if you think you'll forget all this? Then you can sum it all up in this rhythmical rap...

> **If you're rapping very quickly 'cos you're the speedy sort**
> **You gotta keep your syllables all snappy and quite short**
> **But when you go slow**
> **Don't sound wrong...**
> **Make those syllables**
> **Proud and LONG!**

It's ... like ... er ...

Now we'll take a look at imagery, personification, the pathetic fallacy, and onomatopoeia – and don't be put off by the jargon. It's easier than you think.

1. Imagery

Imagery means comparisons (only it's a posher word and impresses examiners). A comparison is when a writer tells us what something or someone is LIKE.

We all use comparisons all the time.

It's as easy as falling off a log.

My boyfriend looks like Brad Pitt.

The exam was a nightmare.

The speakers really mean:

It's extremely easy.

My boyfriend is good-looking, in an American, hunky sort of way.

The exam was very hard.

Generally the comparisons work better as communication tools because they bring pictures to the mind of the listener. The idea of someone falling off a log might make us smile, the idea of Brad Pitt might make us smile even more (if you're female) and an exam being a nightmare says it all – it's so much more concise and informative than going into specific detail. And these are everyday comparisons. When you try that little bit harder and come up with original comparisons, the effect is even better.

- Barry Hines, in his novel *Kes*, describes *"loosely crumpled paper towels"* as *"a bag of cream puffs"*.

- Richard Kell, in the poem "Pigeons", describes them as having *"heads like tiny hammers"* (which) *"tap at imaginary nails"*.

- D H Lawrence, in his novel *Sons and Lovers*, says of a man about to fight, "*He felt his whole body unsheath itself like a claw.*"

These comparisons are slightly harder to unravel, but when you do (see below), and you see why the writer chose them, it's as exciting as solving a puzzle. (Hey! I just used a comparison!)

This section is going to look at different sorts of comparisons (imagery) and show you how to comment on them.

Similes

A simile is a comparison that uses the words "like" or "as". Look carefully at its spelling – there's only two "i"s in "simile". It reminds you of the word "similar". So a simile shows you two things that are similar to each other.

> **He hugged me**
> **<u>like a boa constrictor</u>.**
>
> **He strutted across the**
> **stage <u>like a peacock</u>.**
>
> **The sharp knife sliced**
> **through his flesh**
> **<u>as easily as if it were butter</u>.**

It's easy to spot similes because they always have the key words "like" or "as" in them.

Now try fitting some together yourself. Try to match up these simile openings with their conclusions.

1. Her mournful sigh was   **a)** like a dieter afraid of missing lunch

2. The salesman grinned at me

3. My aunt frowned

4. She flew anxiously along the street

b) like the dying fall of a tired breeze.

c) like an eager puppy-dog.

d) as sternly as if I was removing my underwear in public.

Answers on page 200.

The world's worst similes

He was as tall as a six-foot-three-inch tree.

Her hair glistened in the rain like nostril hair after a sneeze.

The hailstones leaped from the pavement just like maggots when you fry them in hot grease.

Long separated by cruel fate, the star-crossed lovers raced across the grassy meadow towards each other like two freight trains, one having left Euston at 6.36 pm travelling at 55 mph, the other from Birmingham New Street at 4.19 pm at a speed of 35 mph.

John and Mary had never met. They were like two hummingbirds who had also never met.

His thoughts tumbled in his head like Y-fronts in a dryer.

Metaphors

A metaphor is a comparison *without* the words "like" or "as". Because those words are missing, metaphors can be more difficult to find.

" I'm sure there's a metaphor under here somewhere."

However, a metaphor is still a comparison.

The exam was a nightmare.

This is a metaphor. The exam, as difficult as it might have been, was not actually a nightmare. The candidate did not go to sleep one night and twist and turn as a killer exam stalked the mean streets with a sawn-off shotgun, hell-bent on slaughtering him. He simply found himself unable to tackle all parts of a particularly testing examination paper.

A good sign that a metaphor is being used is that a statement is made (the exam was a nightmare) that cannot be taken literally.

I stood on the stage and looked into a <u>sea of faces</u>.

(The faces were not wet with fishes swimming in them.)

Thoughts <u>buzzed</u> in my head.

(My thoughts didn't actually make a humming sound like bees – there were just a lot of them.)

Its squeal was the <u>rending of metal</u>.

This is from Ted Hughes' poem, "View of a Pig". The pig wasn't literally tearing metal apart (difficult!) but his squeal was like the poet's idea of the sound of metal being torn apart.

If you like, think of metaphors as hidden comparisons, and similes as obvious comparisons. But in both sorts, one thing is being compared to another.

Great! So all I have to do is find the similes and metaphors and I'm finished. Easy enough.

Ah no! Finding them is only 25 per cent of the work. Once you've found them, you have to comment on them.

Comment on them? Like, how you do that?

Say how they work and why they're effective. Let me explain...

How to Comment on Imagery
In both similes and metaphors, one thing is being compared to another.

My uncle drinks like a fish.

In this simile, the way your uncle drinks is being compared to the way a fish drinks. But wait. Fishes don't drink out of glasses or cups. They're surrounded by water and are taking it in all the time. So perhaps your uncle is always drinking, and drinking vast quantities. Of sea water? Doubtful. Beer is much more likely. Neither does your uncle have scales or gills like a fish. So the quality that a fish and your uncle have in common is that drinking is second nature to them. *Your uncle is a heavy drinker, and so is a fish.*

My goldfish likes Carling Special Brew.

Shut up. The art of commenting sensibly on imagery is firstly to work out exactly what it is the two things have in common.

Let's go back to the pigeons that were mentioned earlier...

**...heads like tiny hammers
Tap at imaginary nails...**

Thing being described
The movement of pigeons'
heads

The comparison
Tiny hammers tapping
at nails

Note: It's the movement of the pigeons' heads that the poet is interested in here – not their appearance. Pigeons' heads do not look like hammers. The movement the poet is trying to describe is a repetitive, rhythmical tapping. That's the quality the two parts of the comparison have in common.

He felt his whole body unsheath itself like a claw.

Thing being described
The feeling in the man's
body

The comparison
The claw of an animal
coming out of its sheath

It's fairly easy to guess that what is being described here is a man preparing for a fight. His body feels taut and every sense is sharpened. He feels like an animal, vicious and ready for attack.

I don't think I could have got all that.

73

Maybe not. But the trick is to think of how YOU feel when you think about a claw coming out of a sheath. What associations do you have with that action? Use your imagination. Remember that in English Literature anything reasonable that you say that can be backed up by evidence is OK. Splash out a bit!

All right. I'll give it a whirl.

Here's a poem by Alfred, Lord Tennyson, called "The Eagle".

Alfred, Lord Tennyson? Lord's a funny middle name.

It wasn't his middle name. Queen Victoria made him a lord because she rated him so highly. Towards the end of her life they were neighbours on the Isle of Wight. When Queen Vic was getting over the death of her husband Prince Albert, she said Tennyson's poem "In Memoriam" was a tremendous comfort.

Weird.

Tennyson was quite weird. He had a long, flowing beard and suffered from bouts of insanity. But his poetry's pretty cool. Here's "The Eagle".

> He clasps the crag with crooked hands;
> Close to the sun in lonely lands,
> Ring'd with the azure world, he stands.
> The wrinkled sea beneath him crawls;
> He watches from his mountain walls,
> And like a thunderbolt he falls.

I think I get this. It's a description of an eagle. He's looking down from a mountain.

Absolutely right. So where is the imagery?

You mean the similes and metaphors?

75

I do.

OK. "With crooked hands" –
because eagles don't have hands, they
have claws. "The wrinkled sea" – because
it's usually faces or sheets which are
wrinkled. "Like a thunderbolt" –
because the eagle isn't actually a
thunderbolt.

Well done. "Like a thunderbolt" is a simile; the other two are metaphors. So what can you find to say about them?

Ah – this is
the hard bit. Was
that the phone ringing?
I think I'd better go
and answer it.

Coward. The eagle's swoop is described as a thunderbolt. How does that make you feel?

Well, thunderbolts are dead quick, aren't they? And sudden. And it might cause damage. And they're scary.

OK. So now express those ideas in proper sentences.

The eagle's swoop is described as a thunderbolt because the bird dives down suddenly. This is a frightening image. It makes me think of the thing it's swooping down to kill. It will be completely destroyed.

Brilliant! You're a whizz at this. What about that "wrinkled sea".

Right. The sea is described as wrinkled because it's the waves seen from very high up – they look like wrinkles on a sheet or on a face. You get the feeling of the vast distance between the eagle and the sea.

You're a born critic! Now try "with crooked hands".

The hands are really the eagle's claws. I can't think of anything more to say.

Who normally has hands?

People. Human beings. Oh, right. So the eagle is being described as a human.

And it makes him seem more powerful.

I see. But the phone really is ringing, chirruping like a bird in the dawn chorus. This gives the impression that the phone is a bird with a life of its own...

You've got it!

Don't worry if you find it hard to say things about the images you meet. It's a matter of confidence and practice. Remember the examiner is interested in your personal response. *In English Literature GCSE you never get marks knocked off for wrong ideas, but only marks added on for right ideas.* If you feel it's relevant, say it!

2. Personification

Personification is when something is described as if it were a person – as if it were human.

> **The shabby, down-at-heel house, seemed to be propped up by its neighbours. As I approached it a light winked at me from one of upstairs windows. I pressed the doorbell which gave an outraged ring...**

Here the writer is imagining the house as a living creature. It's "shabby" and "down-at-heel" which makes it sound like a tramp.

The way it's propped up by its neighbours (other houses) makes it sound like a drunken tramp. The light going on upstairs is described as a "wink" and the doorbell was "outraged" to be rung, which is a human emotion.

Hold on a minute – this sounds more like an image to me. The writer's comparing the house to a person.

Indeed he is. And that's personification – a hidden comparison to a human. If you like, it's a special sort of metaphor.

Oh, right. Then it's quite easy, isn't it? Let's go on to the next one.

Except we've only done half the work. Recognizing a device – in this case, personification, is one thing, but now we've got to say *why* a writer uses it and *what effect it has*.

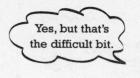
Yes, but that's the difficult bit.

Exactly. But look at it this way:

Action	Effect
You put sugar in your tea.	It makes it sweet.
You put petrol in your car.	It makes it go.
You wear designer jeans.	You're a babe magnet.

It's just the same with literary devices – a writer uses them not for their own sake, but for a purpose.

Action	Effect
The writer uses personification.	It makes something human. It gives it a certain characters. It might make us laugh. Etc...

For example:

...the first growl of winter's anger...

In this use of personification, winter is described as growling. This has the effect of making the winter sound alive and fierce.

...the warm sun caressed her face and soothed her troubled spirit...

Here the sun is seen almost as a mother, caressing and soothing the girl. This creates a calm atmosphere.

81

Ha! You didn't use the word "personification".

That's OK. It's actually more important to comment on the effect of a device than name it. Too much jargon in your essay can clutter it or make the examiner think you're a show-off.

Actually that's good to know, because if I'm not sure whether something is personification or not, I don't have to commit myself.

Precisely.

Hey – I'm getting the hang of this!

3. Pathetic fallacy

Pathetic fallacy is a strange name for an everyday writer's device – when a writer makes an inanimate thing such as the weather match the mood of a character...

Try this quick quiz.

1. You wake up. You look out of your window. The sun is shining, the sky is an unbroken blue and birds are singing. How do you feel?

a) In a good mood.

b) Depressed – because you've got to stay in and revise.

c) Terrified – this is clearly evidence of global warming.

2. You wake up. Rain is lashing down, the sky is a dismal grey and there is the warning rumble of thunder. How do you feel?

a) Depressed.

b) In a good mood – you've just bought a snazzy new umbrella.

c) Terrified – you promised your parents you'd bring in the deckchairs last night and you forgot.

3. You wake up. In the distance you see a funnel-shaped wind steadily approaching, and your bedside radio warns of an imminent tornado. How do you feel?

a) Terrified.

b) Depressed – if it had arrived last week you wouldn't have had to take your biology test.

c) In a good mood – the wind always does interesting things to your hair.

Answers:

All c)s and b)s? You don't take these quizzes very seriously, do you?

All a)s: You are reassuringly normal, just like 99 per cent of the population. The weather affects your mood. In fact, there are even people who get clinically depressed when there isn't any sunshine.

Writers know that there is a relationship between weather and mood, and they often make the weather they describe match the mood they're trying to convey, or even give some indication of the mood of a character. If a writer tells you what the weather is like, they're not auditioning for a spot after the news on TV – they're giving you important inside information.

Actually, I can see that. But why isn't the device called "matching weather"?

OK. The name was made up by a Victorian writer who didn't rate this device very highly, and the name has stuck. But you can impress your friends at parties!

"it's lovely pathetic fallacy tonight, isn't it?"

Now take a look at the pathetic fallacy in action.

> **The rain set early in to-night,**
> **The sullen wind was soon awake,**
> **It tore the elm-tops down for spite,**
> **And did its worse to vex the lake:**
> **I listened with heart fit to break.**

Not an evening for a picnic, evidently. The weather is "sullen" (a touch of personification there!), full of "spite". It "did its worse to vex the lake". And how is the speaker of this poem feeling? His heart is "fit to break". In fact, it gets better. This extract is taken from Robert Browning's poem "Porphyria's Lover" (as is the earlier extract on page 62). Later in the poem the speaker turns out to be a psychotic murderer who strangles the woman he loves. The description of the weather could even be said to prepare us for that.

TOP TIP
Since not all novels or stories, plays or poems are set outside, writers might instead make the décor of a room or the objects in it match the character or mood. You'll get credit if you can spot that.

4. Onomatopoeia

Yer what?

Onomatopoeia – pronounced "onno-matter-peeyer". Or you can remember it by using an old music hall joke: Q. Where is the cat sitting? A. On a mat up 'ere. To learn the spelling you'll need to break the word into sections and learn them separately. Ono/mato/poe/ia.

Fine. So what does it mean, then?

The spelling is harder than its meaning. It means a word which sounds exactly like its meaning. For example:

Miaow –   sounds like the cry of a cat (try taping your cat if you don't believe me)

Hiccup –   sounds like the noise you make when you drink your cola too fast – so does **burp**

Wheeze –   all of those of you with asthma will recognize this word as onomatopoeiac

Crash, chirrup, smack, etc.

The effect of onomatopoeiac words is simply to help you hear the thing being described as well as think about it. You get double your money's worth.

Two points of caution:

1. Don't say a word is onomatopoeiac unless you are absolutely sure. Some words are far from sounding like the thing they are. "Snog", for example…

2. If you are in an exam and are not sure whether the poem you are studying contains onomatopoeia or not, do NOT say the word aloud to test it....

Designer Lit

Remember to step back from the literature you're studying and take a look at the overall design. In this section we'll examine structure and contrast, and smooth out the subject of irony!

1. Structure

As word order is to a sentence, so structure is to a whole story, poem, play or even a novel. It really matters what order things are told in. Look at this joke:

A sandwich walks into a bar and asks for half a pint of lager. "Sorry," says the barman. "We don't serve food here."

Here's the same joke told in a different order.

The barman said, "we don't serve food here" when he was asked for half a pint of lager by a sandwich.

Putting the punch line first is not a good idea. A joke needs an element of suspense to work. (A joke is really just a very short story.) The same rules apply to stories, plays and novels. You wouldn't choose to read a crime novel that began "The butler did it." Writers have to give some thought to the order they tell things in. And that order isn't necessarily beginning-middle-end.

Take this storyline:

Beginning. **A very hard up, unemployed man, Charlie, goes for a walk. He sees a fifty pound note on the pavement.** *Middle:* **He picks it up as no one is around.**

87

He is very tempted to keep it. However, his conscience gets the better of him, and he decides to take the note to the Police Station. He hands in the note, and as he does so he sees a notice on the wall advertising a telephone operating job in the station. *End:* Charlie applies and gets the job.

A writer telling this story has three alternatives.

a) He could tell the story as it is above, from the beginning, through the middle, to the end.

b) He could start with the end – Charlie is busy operating the police switchboard, then thinks back to how he got the job.

c) He could start in the middle – Charlie is asking himself whether he should keep the note or not (a moment of dramatic indecision), then thinks back to how he found it, before the story moves forward through his decision and its consequences.

a) is clear and straightforward; **b)** raises an interesting question as to how Charlie got the job; **c)** opens with a moment of drama and delays the outcome as long as possible. Each version has advantages and drawbacks. As a student of literature, you have to work out what these are.

Think about the storylines in books you've come across. *Macbeth*, for example, opens at the beginning. *An Inspector Calls* starts in the middle. *To Kill a Mockingbird* begins at the end.

Beginning → middle → end	is clear but could be predictable.
Middle → beginning → end	allows you to start at the most interesting moment, but could be confusing.
End → beginning → middle	gives a sense of inevitability (we know what happens at the end) but gives the game away.

Also, have a look at how much of the text is devoted to each section – writers don't necessarily spend the same amount of time on beginning and middle and end. Get a feel for the overall design of a work of literature.

Hey! This design thing is a bit like a football match. You can score goals at the beginning, which is great if it's your team, but the match can get boring, or in the middle, which raises the tension, or at the end, like Man United against Bayern Munich when they won the treble. Now that was some game.

Rather like a tragedy by Shakespeare, when most of the deaths come at the end, or a comedy, when all the marriages come at the end.

Trust you to bring literature into everything!

89

I find writing a summary of a text helps me see the pattern of it – and it helps it stick in my mind for the exam.

I hate texts that give the end away at the beginning – I mean – what's the point of reading it?

I like the challenge of reading a novel that you have to piece together because the writer takes you backwards and forwards in time – it's like solving a crossword puzzle.

2. Contrast

Contrast occurs when two very different things are placed next to each other.

I knew that. Like my white T-shirt and black denims.

Yes. That's contrast.

Or you can adjust the contrast on a TV screen, which sharpens the picture because the black stands out from the white more!

That's also contrast.

Or when I stand next to my mate Sam who's nine inches shorter than me.

91

I suppose you could get away with saying that was a contrast too. But I want to talk about contrasts in literature.

When you put two very different things together, each one tends to stand out more. That's why writers use contrast a lot. They might use it within a sentence or line of verse, but more often it's used on a bigger scale – you might get two characters in a novel who contrast, one being good, and the other a nasty piece of work. To take some simple examples…

- In Shakespeare's *Macbeth*, there is a contrast between good (Duncan, Malcolm) and evil (Macbeth, Lady Macbeth, the witches).

- In Steinbeck's *Of Mice And Men*, there is a contrast at the end between Lennie's touching faith that he'll get to feed the rabbits, and the stark reality that George is about to shoot him.

- In Harper Lee's *To Kill A Mockingbird*, there is a contrast between the way the children imagine Boo Radley to be, and the way he actually is.

- In J B Priestley's *An Inspector Calls*, there is a contrast between Eva Smith and virtually every other character.

These are just four typical GCSE set texts: see if you can work out how contrast is used in your set texts. Then see if you can link the use of contrast to the effect it has. Sometimes contrast can make us laugh – think of comedians like Lily Savage and the contrast between her husky voice and over-the-top hair and make up, and between her female dress, and the fact we know she's a man. Shakespeare achieves a similar effect when the beautiful fairy queen Titania is flirting like mad with Bottom with his ass's head in *A Midsummer Night's Dream*.

At other times contrast can make us feel sad or even angry – have you ever been sickened by reading a newspaper and seeing reports of a famine on one page, and an advertisement for a new, expensive restaurant on the other? In Mildred Taylor's *Roll Of Thunder, Hear My Cry* contrast is used in a similar way to highlight inequality between the black and white populations.

Contrast is a very common literary device, and easy to find, but also easy to overlook. But now you've read this, you won't be the one to overlook it!

3. Irony

Irony is when a writer says one thing, but means the opposite.

What's the point of that? Like, wouldn't it be easier for a writer to say what they mean in the first place? Like, if my mum asked me what I wanted for dinner and I said fish and chips, but I really meant kebab and salad, she'd give me fish and chips.

Writers do have good reasons for saying the opposite of what they mean. In fact, it's not only writers who do it:

Your father, on unpacking all the picnic gear and seeing it's raining again:

Your teacher, on hearing you read aloud in the world's most boring voice:

You, on listening to your little sister attempting to tell a not very funny joke:

Sarcasm is very close to irony. You wouldn't ever say a writer was being sarcastic (unless he met you and made a nasty personal remark) but you might want to say he was being ironic.

I've thought of another problem. How can I tell if a writer is being ironic? If he says 'Joe Bloggs entered the room' for all I know Joe Bloggs didn't enter the room – the author was being ironic.

I sympathize with your anxiety. In fact, irony isn't always easy to spot. Even the best students can miss it. This is because with spoken sarcasm the tone of voice is the big giveaway. With the written word, there's no tone of voice to help you. Instead you have to tune in to the tone of the writing, which is much, much trickier. But with this book to help you, you'll have a head start in irony detection.

Read this passage:

> John Forrest, the new vicar, was the man responsible for the sudden religious revival in the village of Cobden. His devotion to his flock was exemplary; his efforts to fill the pews were nothing short of heroic. Never had Cobden seen such an earnest Christian. In particular, the young ladies of Cobden had never seen a vicar so young, with such chiselled features, such an appealing lock of hair that fell on to his forehead, or a smile that melted each and every female heart.

The first three sentences paint John Forrest as an "earnest Christian". The fourth sentence, however, tells us that the real reason everyone was going to church was to take a gander at this young hunk who sounds suspiciously like a film star. So when the writer talks in the first three sentences about him as spearheading a religious revival, she is being ironic. She really means everyone fancied him and he was probably a flirt. The clue to the irony is the detail in the fourth sentence about his appearance. You, the student, have to be a bit of a detective.

Here's the opening of a famous poem that uses irony in a very striking way. It's by Sir John Betjeman.

> Sir John Betjeman lived from 1906 to 1984. He was a very popular poet – well-known for his skill in rhyming. He was Poet Laureate and also a great fan of Coronation Street!

> Come friendly bombs and fall on Slough!
> It isn't fit for humans now,
> There isn't grass to graze a cow.
> Swarm over, Death!
>
> Come, bombs, and blow to smithereens
> Those air-conditioned bright canteens,
> Tinned fruit, tinned meat, tinned milk, tinned beans,
> Tinned minds, tinned breath.

Apparently Betjeman is asking bombs to come and destroy Slough, in particular its canteens, processed food and people with bad breath. As you might imagine, this poem is not very popular in Slough.

However, when you realize Betjeman is using irony, the verses read differently. He doesn't really want Slough to be wiped off the face of the earth, but he does want to see Slough restored to the way it used to be before modernization occurred. What he doesn't like is faceless modern towns. There's a hint in "There isn't grass to graze a cow" that Betjeman prefers old-fashioned rural life. His true meaning is that we modernize towns at our peril. If you get hold of the rest of the poem you'll see that clearly.

The clue to the irony is the very extreme way Betjeman expresses himself. Slough isn't that bad – believe me, I've been there.

OK. Now look at the opening of Jane Austen's novel, *Pride and Prejudice*.

It is a truth universally acknowledged that a single man in possession of a good fortune must be in want of a wife.

Stop right there. Think about what you've just read. *Does* a rich, single man always need a wife? I think not. A rich, single man is probably capable of having a perfectly good time without a wife. So who is it who thinks that a rich, single man must be looking for a wife? Read the next sentence.

> However little known the feelings or views of such a man may be on his first entering a neighbourhood, this truth is so well fixed in the minds of the surrounding families, that he is considered as the rightful property of some one or other of their daughters...

So it wasn't a "truth universally acknowledged", after all. It's just that families with young, single daughters wanted it to be true and act as if it was. So in her first sentence Jane Austen is deliberately saying the opposite of what she means – she is being ironic!

Why? Pick the reasons below that seem the most likely to you.

a) She wanted to try to trip the reader up as she didn't like readers.

b) She wanted to make the reader smile at people's desire to get their daughters married off.

c) She wanted to slow the reader down and make them think about what they've just read.

d) She wanted to show off.

e) She wanted to start her novel in an amusing way to show there'll be more fun later on.

f) She can't decide whether it is true that a single man in possession of a good fortune wants a wife or not.

Answers on page 200.

4. Dramatic irony

Dramatic irony is when the audience or reader *knows more* about the situation the characters are in, than the characters themselves.

Don't confuse dramatic irony with irony – they are two separate things. If you like, dramatic irony is an irony of situation, rather than irony with words.

So if I take my umbrella with me because I think it's going to rain, and the sun shines all day, that's ironic, isn't it?

Yes – that would be dramatic irony in a play, if the audience had previously seen the weather forecast and knew it was going to be fine. A dramatist who uses dramatic irony a lot is —

Don't tell me. Shakespeare.

You're getting the hang of this. Yes, it's Shakespeare.

- In *Macbeth*, Duncan exclaims how pleasant Macbeth's castle seems to him, but the audience knows Macbeth is plotting to kill him in there.

- In *Romeo and Juliet*, when Juliet's father insists she marries Paris, the audience knows she's already married to Romeo.

- In *A Midsummer Night's Dream*, Titania thinks she's fallen in love with the world's most handsome man, but the audience knows she's been enchanted and it's really Bottom with an ass's head.

Whichever Shakespeare play you're studying, there's bound to be some dramatic irony. Ask yourself what the effect of the dramatic irony is.

- In *Macbeth*, we feel fear and sympathy for Duncan, and are more aware of Macbeth's treachery.

- In *Romeo And Juliet*, we feel increased fear and anticipation for Juliet – a strange mixture of emotions, because on the one

101

hand we think she'll be safe, but on the other we are scared that her father will be furious.

- In *A Midsummer Night's Dream*, we find the dramatic irony very funny – we laugh. Only we and Shakespeare know what's really going on and that makes us feel powerful.

Look out for dramatic irony in other, more modern, plays and even in soap operas – especially in soap operas! If you've read in the Speedy TV Guide that there's going to be an earthquake in *Brookend Street Farm*, as you watch all the characters going about their normal business, completely unaware of the impending catastrophe, well, that's dramatic irony too.

Putting it all together

In fact, the techniques writers use are endless. If we were to try to list them all, we'd probably run out of paper! Some writers use *repetition* to emphasize a point, or *lists and statistics* to create a matter-of-fact feel. They *vary the length of sentences* for dramatic impact, they use *word-play* such as puns, or *anti-climax* – there are almost as many writers' devices as there are writers.

The important thing for you is to be aware of them as you study a piece of literature. Understanding the content and meaning of a work of literature is only half the work; looking at how it is written is the other half.

Now test yourself. Here's a poem by Ted Hughes, a British poet who died in 1998. He was the Poet Laureate, and well-known for his violent nature poems. Here he is describing a jaguar confined to a cage. The jaguar is enraged at his captivity and is striding to and fro in the cage. First Ted Hughes sets the scene...

The Jaguar
The apes yawn and adore their fleas in the sun.
The parrots shriek as if they were on fire, or strut
Like cheap tarts to attract the stroller with the nut.

Fatigued with indolence, tiger and lion

Lie still as the sun. The boa-constrictor's coil
Is a fossil. Cage after cage seems empty, or
Stinks of sleepers from the breathing straw.
It might be painted on a nursery wall.

But who runs like the rest past these arrives
At a cage where the crowd stands, stares, mesmerised,
As a child at a dream, at a jaguar hurrying enraged
Through prison darkness after the drills of his eyes

On a short fierce fuse. Not in boredom –
The eye satisfied to be blind in fire,
By the bang of blood in the brain deaf the ear –
He spins from the bars, but there's no cage to him

More than to the visionary his cell:
His stride is wildernesses of freedom:
The world rolls under the long thrust of his heel.
Over the cage floor the horizons come.

This is a difficult poem, especially towards the end. Before you
started reading this book, you might not have had a clue where
to begin. But now you should be unafraid. If you look back over
the writers' techniques in this chapter – we've looked at...

- Diction
- Alliteration
- Word order
- Rhythm
- Imagery
- Personification
- Pathetic fallacy
- Onomatopoeia
- Structure
- Contrast
- Irony
- Dramatic irony

...you'll see immediately that not all of them are used here, but
some are. Yes, Ted Hughes does some interesting things with
diction, imagery, word order, structure, alliteration,
onomatopoeia, rhythm, contrast and dramatic irony. Wow! You

don't even need to understand all of the poem before you start writing!

You read the poem again, and label it in rough like this:

The Jaguar

The apes yawn and adore their fleas in the sun.

onomatopoeia = makes more vivid

The parrots shriek as if they were on fire, or strut

simile - a painful sound and re-emphasises heat

Like cheap tarts to attract the stroller with the nut.

simile - shocking to think of parrots as prostitutes!

Fatigued with indolence, tiger and lion

What does this mean?

Lie still as the sun. The boa-constrictor's coil

repetition of sun - it's being stressed

Is a fossil. Cage after cage seems empty, or

Metaphor - stresses the snake is absolutely still   *rhythm - long syllables slow verse down as animals are sleeping*

Stinks of sleepers from the breathing straw.

diction - an unexpected, violent word

It might be painted on a nursery wall.

contrast between sleeping animals and enraged jaguar - a two part structure to the poem

alliteration

But who runs like the rest past these arrives

104

alliteration

At a cage where the crowd stands, stares,
mesmerised,

diction - the crowd sounds as if they're under a spell

word order, suspense, we have to wait to see what's in the cage

As a child at a dream, at a jaguar hurrying enraged

Through prison darkness after the drills of his eyes

diction - cage like a cell, like the jaguar's being punished?

On a short fierce fuse. Not in boredom –
The eye satisfied to be blind in fire,
By the bang of blood in the brain deaf the ear –

triple alliteration, an explosive sound and short syllables = fast pace

dramatic irony that crowd don't realise how the jaguar feels

He spins from the bars, but there's no cage to him

?? don't understand, but maybe the jaguar's trying to imagine he's somewhere else - like you can never really trap a jaguar

More than to the visionary his cell:
His stride is wildernesses of freedom:
The world rolls under the long thrust of his heel.
Over the cage floor the horizons come.

Now you have all the raw material you need to write a first-class essay. In fact you're almost ready to turn to chapter four, where you'll find everything you ever needed to know about how to write a stonking literature essay. But first, a few more thoughts about those three types of literature: poetry, prose and drama…

Plays, prose, poetry ... write all about it!

All GCSE candidates study three **genres** (kinds) of literature:

- Prose (novels, short stories, etc)
- Drama (plays)
- Poetry

Although they have a lot in common, each genre has its own special considerations, and you need to be aware of these before you settle down to study one of them. If you'd never played Monopoly before, you wouldn't just start playing – you'd need to find out the rules first. It's the same with literature.

Novel gazing

What's a novel? Here are seven books – and only two of them are novels. Which two?

1. *Short Stories of Our Time*, Ed. D R Barnes
2. *The Rupert Bear Annual*
3. *How to Cook*, Delia Smith
4. *The Complete Works of Alfred, Lord Tennyson*
5. *Gone With The Wind*, Margaret Mitchell
6. *The Concise Oxford English Dictionary*
7. *1984*, George Orwell

Even if you haven't read **1**, you can see it's a collection of short stories, therefore it's not a novel. A novel is **continuous**.

2 is also a collection of stories and not a novel. That it's about Rupert Bear doesn't disqualify it, though. Many excellent novels are written for children.

If you want to know how to boil an egg, read Delia Smith (**3**). This book of recipes and instructions (a bestseller) will give you the facts about cooking. It's not a novel because a novel has to be **fiction** (not true).

4 is a very long collection of poetry, as Tennyson was a poet. All his poems are arranged in lines and verses. This book is definitely not a novel because a novel is almost always written in **prose**, i.e. sentences arranged in continuous succession, broken by paragraphs.

Hooray! **5** is truly a novel. *Gone With The Wind,* as well as being a very successful feature film, was also a long, continuous prose fiction – A NOVEL. It's colourful and romantic and I doubt whether you'd be asked to study it on your GCSE syllabus.

6 is a dictionary – useful for reading novels and even writing novels, but it clearly isn't a novel.

7 is also a novel, even though it's also a year! George Orwell wrote in 1948 and he was warning people in the 1940s how life might turn out in the future if they let dictators flourish. Even though the book is futuristic, it's still a novel – it's a long, continuous prose fiction.

Now you know what a novel is, let the examiner know that you know. Never refer in an essay to a novel (or a play or poem) you study as a *book*. Call it a novel (or a play or poem). A book is simply pages bound up between two covers – and not necessarily a work of literature.

A tour of the novel

Welcome on board the Excelsior Touring
company's luxurious double-decker,
for your tour of the novel with commentaries
in three different languages.
Bienvenue...

As we start off, I must ask you to ensure
that your seatbelts are fastened. Thank you.
Now, if you look to your right between those
two large buildings you'll see a PLOT...

Plot

In a novel, a plot is more than just the story. In a story, one thing happens after another, not necessarily for any particular reason:

> I pushed my trolley around the supermarket on Saturday morning. I put in it some cornflakes, some cola, a packet of washing powder, some oranges and sticking plaster. Then I went to the checkout to have my purchases scanned and I paid for them with my debit card. Then I put my shopping in two plastic bags and carried them to the car. Then I put them in the boot of my car, got in to the car, and drove off.

That's a story. Now compare this.

> It was Saturday morning and I was pushing my trolley round the supermarket. Looking along the shelves for a cheap washing powder I ran my trolley into a woman's ankle. She began screaming at me for being so careless, and pointing out her bleeding ankle. I told her she was a silly old bag and walked off, but inwardly I was raging. I had to wait for ages at the checkout because the old woman in front of me was counting the correct change. I could feel myself getting angrier and angrier. Then as I was driving out of the supermarket the same woman whose ankle I'd hurt overtook me. Right, I thought, that's it. So I chased her down the dual carriageway, went through a red light and straight into the side of a lorry carrying washing powder.

That's a story *with a plot*. When you have a plot, one thing happens *because* another thing has happened. *Because* the narrator was angry, he or she indulged in a spot of road rage and almost killed him- or herself.

It's the same with a plot in a play or novel. Take *Of Mice And Men*. Lennie is killed at the end *because* he has accidentally killed a woman *because* he liked stroking soft things *because* he was simple-minded.

Watch to see how a writer uses plot to create suspense by leaving clues or cliffhangers. Most importantly, looking at the plot will bring you close to the heart of the novel, and you'll be able to work out the message of the book. In Jane Austen's *Pride And Prejudice*, Lizzie Bennet and her sister Jane, who are good characters, get the men of their dreams, while Lydia, who is shallow, ends up with a shallow husband. Mary and Kitty Bennet, who are plain and foolish, end up without husbands at all. So the good women always get the guy! In William Golding's *Lord Of The Flies*, the chaos at the end of the novel shows us that boys, left alone without adults, will turn into animals. Civilisation doesn't last very well in a crisis, says Golding.

Think about the novel you're reading, and see if you can work out what the author is trying to tell you through the plot...

I hope you enjoyed that rather intricate plot, and have learned something by it. On your left you can see a fine old building which once housed the Corn Exchange. And now, if you all turn to the right and look just beyond the hump-backed bridge, you'll see a rather attractive theme...

Theme

In music, a theme is a recurring tune. Go to the cinema and listen to the soundtrack of any film, and you'll hear a theme.

In the entertainment industry, a theme park is a place where all the rides relate in different ways to an idea – you can have American adventure theme parks, medieval theme parks, a Disney theme park...

In literature, a theme is a recurring idea that is treated in different ways by the author. In a novel (or a play) a theme might be prejudice, bringing up children, kingship, evil, relationships, love, culture clashes – almost anything.

For example, in Harper Lee's *To Kill a Mockingbird*, one important theme is prejudice. We read about colour prejudice in the trial of Tom Robinson, as well as the sort of prejudice you get in small towns where everyone likes to label everybody else. You also get prejudice based on class.

TOP TIP
If you're expected to write an essay on one of your set texts, you might very well be asked to write about a theme. Check you know what the themes in your set texts are. And remember – all is not what it themes...

Now look down as we pass the hotel on your left
and you'll see an old man wearing full military
uniform except for his McDonald's baseball cap.
He's a bit of a local character...

Character

Every novel has characters, and studying them is one of the single
most important things you do when you get to know your GCSE
novels. See page 37 on how to write a character sketch.

Straight ahead of us, as we
turn left, you can see the Jubilee
Park, planted by William
Aubretia, the renowned
gardener. It's a beautiful place,
especially in spring and
summer, with its secluded
glades, exquisite roses and
ornate pavilions. It provides a
wonderful setting for...

Setting

Every novel is set in a certain time and place. Sometimes the time and place can be imaginary (the twenty-third century, the planet Zog), but there is always a time and place.

In some novels the time and place can be very important, because the writer wants to relate the theme to them. Think about the time and place in your novel. Why has the novelist chosen them? Is a lot of detail given about them? Why?

Don't just skip descriptions – they're usually there for a purpose.

> **TOP TIP**
> If you need to write about mood and atmosphere, a description of the setting is a very good place to start.

Look at this:

> **The garden was still, still as death. Not a twig, not a leaf moved. The moon was obscured by a passing cloud, and all that could be seen was the black bulk of the trees and bushes. Suddenly there was a rustle as a flying thing emerged from the tree, with the baby face and bony wings of a bat...**

Is this setting a good opening for a story about...

a) an embezzlement scandal in the City?
b) a birthday surprise?
c) a night of horror and the supernatural?
d) a first date?

c) is clearly the right answer. Every detail of the setting creates a spooky mood – the dark, the silence, the sudden appearance of the bat. There is an atmosphere of foreboding... A chill runs down your spine... Help!

How to make a drama out of a crisis
In this section, there are some thoughts on how to study a play.

Yeah, but really a play is like studying a novel, innit? I mean, you've got your characters, your themes, your plot, your setting—

Very true – except the setting is usually in the stage directions.

OK, so the setting is usually in the stage directions. But otherwise it's just the same.

It is the same, but it can also be very different. Take a look at this problem page…

"I like reading plays in class because it's not as boring as usual. But when I have to write about the play, I don't know what to write because it's just all people talking. Please help. If I get a low grade at GCSE my parents will be so disappointed."

We can learn a lot about character by studying what people say. In your case, you sometimes find English Literature lessons boring, which could suggest your heart isn't in it. You also seem to think you're doing GCSE for your parents rather than for yourself. And I have deduced all this simply from reading what you've said. I have seen the *subtext* in your letter – and this is what you must do when you are writing about plays. Dig below the surface and ask yourself why characters say the things

they do. Make some guesses about what really motivates them. It's a brilliant way of building a character sketch.

"This is not really my problem but my English teacher's. He's suffering from premature hair loss. He has several bald patches and he's only 35. He says it's all my fault because I keep calling Macbeth a book in my essays. But it is a book! It's between two covers. It fits neatly into my backpack!"

You're right – your teacher's hair loss is his problem, not yours. He should have arranged for you to see a production of *Macbeth*. If you study a play at GCSE you should try to see it. Playwrights write plays to be performed, not to be read. If you can't get to the theatre, see a video. See two videos, or three. What you study in lessons is only a script. The finished product is the play itself. Meanwhile, to improve your chances at GCSE, never refer to a play as a book, and never refer to the reader of a play, only the audience. Send your English teacher to a hair restoring clinic and get yourself a season ticket to your local theatre, or join an amateur dramatic society.

"I'm terrified. I've got to sit an exam on my set play, and I can't get it into my head. It all blurs into a mess. How can I remember it? My mum said she'd stand outside the window of my classroom and mime it, but I think that might be cheating."

You're right. That is cheating and not that helpful. Better – when you revise – to think of your play in terms of its acts and scenes. Make a summary of each scene. Draw a quick graph of the action of each act or scene, plotting what happens against an increase in tension.

Don't spend too long on this, but it will help you get a feel for dramatic climax. You'll also see the pattern of the play much more clearly – which is another way of saying you'll have a clear overview, and examiners value clear overviews.

You'll remember the pattern much more easily, and you'll get a feel for a dramatic climax. You'll see how the whole play is structured.

"I like plays, and I can even write OK character sketches. But my problem is that I have a phobia. Every time I read a phrase in an essay title like 'dramatic effect' or 'dramatic impact' or 'dramatic significance' I go all cold and break out into a sweat. My bottom lip quivers and my teeth chatter. I start to hyperventilate and – oh no – it's happening again. I should have never written those words. What can I do?"

Your panic attacks are caused by the fact you don't understand the terms you mention. We all have a fear of the unknown, and one of the best ways to attack fear is by arming yourself with knowledge. Now, take a few deep calming breaths, relax your shoulders where the tension is concentrated, and try to visualize something serene and calm while I explain...

"Dramatic" simply means relating to the play. It does not mean "exciting". Out of the English Literature classroom, "dramatic" can often mean exciting (e.g. the goal was dramatic). But when we refer to literature, "dramatic" simply refers to the play.

Therefore *"dramatic effect"* means the effect of something in the play. For example, you might be asked what is the dramatic effe of a scene where one character threatens another. The answer might be that we learn more about the relationship between both characters, we can see that there might be a violent ending, the tension is increased.

"Dramatic impact" uses the word "dramatic" in exactly the same way, so it means what impact a certain part of the play has on the rest of it. In that part we might learn more about character, find out something about the plot or learn more about the themes.

"Dramatic significance" again simply means what is significant about the part of the play you are looking at.

That's really all there is to it.

Now I shall give you an aromatherapy massage while you listen to some New Age Celtic Mood Music and repeat as your mantra, that dramatic simply means relating to the play, dramatic simply means relating to the play, dramatic simply means relating to the play...

Considering Shakesbore

It's highly unlikely you'll get through your English Literature GCSE without coming across Shakespeare. In fact, you may have even chosen to take English Lit because you once saw a film of a Shakespeare play and thought it was cool. And then your English teacher hands out dog-eared copies of some other play by your man, and you begin to read it in class and realize that **a)** it's nothing like the film, **b)** you don't understand it, **c)** the teacher thinks you understand it and doesn't bother to explain what it means, **d)** you suddenly feel very sleepy, and **e)** it's the end of the lesson and you've got a written homework on the scene you've just missed.

So for all of you (most of you) who have found that studying Shakespeare makes you reach for the Paracetamol, here's the combination to unlock his secrets.

click, click, click, 6...

Everyone finds studying Shakespeare hard. Accept that you'll need to read the text more than once to get its full meaning out. You'll be amazed at how much more you'll understand the second time around. Or even the third. And on each reading it gets more interesting, rather than less interesting. Amazing but true...

click, 5...

Shakespeare wrote *plays* and he would be mortally offended if he knew you read his play and didn't see it. Make sure you see the play you study either on stage or on a video. You'll understand it a whole lot better, and like it more too...

click, 4...

In Shakespeare's day, plays were written partly in verse. It was the tradition. So in order to fit his characters' words into ten syllable lines, Shakespeare compresses the language. This means he sometimes leaves out little words that help you understand what the characters are on about. Get yourself a good edition of your play that explains the difficult bits at the bottom of the page. And remember, most GCSE boards at the moment let you take an annotated version of your text into the exam...

click, 3...

Shakespeare lived and wrote around the end of the sixteenth century when the English language was different from modern English. He used words we no longer use, or spelt them differently, or attached different meanings to them. Be prepared to look up the occasional word in the glossary (dictionary) at the back of your text, or ask your teacher what certain words mean, and write the meaning by the word in your copy of the text. But don't get too carried away with "translating" – the main point is to get to know the text as well as possible.

click, 2...

Shakespeare wasn't just a playwright – he was a poet too. Many of his character's speeches work like poetry, use similes and metaphors, and have different levels of meaning. If you're after a high grade, get switched on to his poetry...

119

click, **1**...

Shakespeare may have lived 400 years ago, but the reason we still see and study his plays is because they're relevant to us today. Get into the habit of connecting what happens in your play to the world you live in. If your parents don't approve of your boyfriend or girlfriend, think *Romeo And Juliet*; if you're studying Hitler and World War Two in history, think *Macbeth*; if you're sickened by racism, think *The Merchant Of Venice*...

6...**5**...**4**...**3**...**2**...**1**... And you've cracked Shakespeare!

Verse and worse
Poetry. You either love it or loathe it.

> I like poetry that rhymes. I think poetry should always rhyme.

Poetry? I don't get it. I can never understand what it's going on about.

I prefer studying poems 'cos they're short. Trouble is, so are my essays.

I like poems that make me laugh like Roger McGough and stuff like that. But all that pre-twentieth century stuff is just weird.

I think poets are ever so clever. I like poetry lessons, but only after the teacher has explained it. I don't think I could study poetry on my own.

Actually, I write my own poems. Well, I do, but they're nothing like what we read in class. I wouldn't show them to anyone, anyway, because they're personal. And they don't rhyme or anything.

Poetry is for wusses.

122

English poetry was first written by and for men — it celebrated victories in battle or expressed loyalty to a battle chief. Later, Elizabethan soldiers wrote poetry — you *had* to if you wanted the court to respect you. The most famous poets who wrote in English — Milton, Pope, Tennyson, Yeats, Eliot — were all male. There's not yet been a female Poet Laureate — so come on, all you girls out there — get writing!

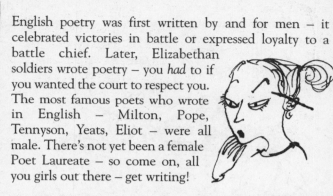

Tricks for reading poetry

If you're one of those people (90 per cent of us) who find studying poetry difficult, it's probably because you're reading poetry in the wrong way.

- Allow the poem time to sink in before you begin to ask yourself what it all means.

- Ask yourself what the mood of the poem is, how the diction and imagery affect you, how the different literary devices work and what effect they have.

- Read the poem aloud to hear the sound of it and feel the rhythm. (Probably best if you only do this when you are on your own...)

Poetry talking points

If you have to study a poem by yourself, first refer to writers' techniques in chapter two (see page 49). Looking for these devices will give you a head start. Then consider:

Rhyme

Does your poem rhyme? Not all poems do; as a general rule, the older the poem, the more likely it is to have a regular rhyme scheme. If you want to describe a rhyme scheme in an essay, use the a,b,c notation.

Little Miss <u>Muffet</u> (a)
Sat on her <u>tuffet</u> (a)
Eating her curds and <u>whey</u>. (b)
Down came a <u>spider</u>. (c)
Who sat down <u>beside her</u>. (c)
And frightened Miss Muffet <u>away</u>. (b)

rhyme scheme = a, a, b, c, c, b

Incy Wincy <u>spider</u> (a)
Climbed up the water-<u>spout</u>. (b)
Down came the <u>rain</u> (c)
And washed the spider <u>out</u>. (b)

rhyme scheme = a, b, c, b

Remember to ask yourself why your poet has chosen a rhyme scheme – to be funny? To sound like a spell or chant? At the end of a poem to round it off properly?

Poetry quiz

See if you can select the correct terminology.

1. A poem with no rhyme and no regular rhythm can be said to be written in . . .
a) free verse.
b) rap.
c) ancient Egyptian.
d) ink.

2. The right word for two consecutive rhyming lines in a poem is a . . .
a) rhyme.
b) triplet.
c) rhyming couplet.
d) Hamlet.

3. The correct term for a paragraph of a poem is a . . .
a) section.
b) verse.
c) stanza.
d) line.

4. A line of poetry that ends with a full stop or other punctuation mark is called. . .

a) Fred.

b) end-stopped.

c) finished.

d) prose.

5. A poem which is fourteen lines long is called. . .

a) a fourteen-line poem.

b) an epic.

c) a limerick.

d) a sonnet.

Answers on page 200.

Now you've familiarized yourself with some poetry jargon, use it. Examiners love to see a word or expression that they can relate to – like "stanza" or "free verse". They will give you lots of lovely marks for them.

Generally, writing about poetry isn't too bad because you usually study poems in class first, and if you take notes, you'll have all the stuff you need to write a devastatingly brilliant essay.

But what if you have to write about a poem you've never seen before…

Unseen poetry trauma

"It started with these nightmares, doctor. I would be innocently eating my tea or taking a walk, and suddenly, out of nowhere, there'd be this poem trying to get me. A big, hulking, hairy poem, one I'd never seen before in my life. I'd begin to sweat. My mind would go blank. Words would swarm around me like killer bees, pressing in, suffocating me..."

126

"I see. Very interesting. Either a birth trauma flashback or a panic attack induced by an unseen poetry assignment. Tell me a little more. What are the thoughts that go through your head when you see a poem that you have to write about unaided?"

"I worry I won't be able to understand it. I worry that I do understand it but I won't find anything to say about it. Then I worry I do understand it and think of something to say about it but it isn't clever enough. Or it's wrong. And my teacher reads what I've written and snorts with sarcastic laughter. And all my mates read the poem and think, hey, that's brilliant, and write really interesting essays. And I don't. And then a huge poem carrying a sixteen-ton weight comes and sits on my chest and stops me breathing – help – I can't stand it!"

"Relax. No poem can come and get you here. You're safe on the psychiatrist's couch. I have to tell you that your fears are very common. No one ever approaches an unseen poem with confidence. The unknown is always frightening. Your anxieties are natural. Next time you meet an unseen poem, take a few deep breaths, and repeat to yourself these positive and true thoughts...

- I will understand some of the poem, and I'm not expected to write about all of it.

- Anything I say with evidence to back me up will be credited.

- All I have to do in a poetry essay is notice things about how the poem is written.

"And if you have read *GCSE English Literature* so far, you will know exactly what techniques to look for, and will be able to find lots of points to make. To give yourself extra confidence, go on to read chapter four, which tells you how to write about literature, and your fears will belong to the past."

"You mean I can actually enjoy reading poetry again one day?"

"I'm certain of it. Ah! That's your hour up. My fee is £134.76 not including VAT."

Your text in context

All GCSE syllabuses ask you to show you know something about the **social and historical background** of your text and the **literary traditions** that influenced it.

It's actually much easier than you think. In fact it's probably the easiest part of studying a text. Not only that, knowing about social and historical background and literary tradition helps you to understand a text.

You will be.

Forget the text for a moment, and think about yourself instead. Ask yourself what are the social and historical factors that have influenced your development?

129

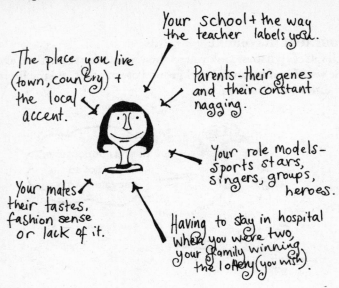

Your school + the way the teacher labels you.

The place you live (town, country) + the local accent.

Parents - their genes and their constant nagging.

Your role models - sports stars, singers, groups, heroes.

Your mates, their tastes, fashion sense or lack of it.

Having to stay in hospital when you were two, your family winning the lottery (you wish).

You wouldn't be the person you are were it not for your parents, your mates, your school, your team winning the cup final or that memorable holiday in Benidorm. And now think about the way you talk. Where did you get your favourite words and phrases from? TV? Your mates? You pick up expressions from people around you.

It's the same with a writer and his or her text. A text doesn't come from nothing or nowhere. It's a product of its times, just as you are. To get to know you, it helps to know your family, where you live, where you go to school, what your favourite music is. To know a text, it helps to know:

- When it was written.
- Where it was written.
- What important events were going on around that time.
- Who the author was.
- What views the author had about the time he or she lived in.
- What other important texts were around at that time.
- Whether they were similar or different to your text.

Not all of these questions will apply to all of your set texts, but most of them will. For example, take George Orwell's *Animal Farm*.

- It was published in 1945.

- It's set in an imaginary land where animals can talk but the writer sees this land as very similar to our own.

- 1945 was the last year of World War Two, but the novel is actually about dictatorship, and gives an interpretation of the events following the Russian Revolution in 1917.

- The author was George Orwell (1903-50). Orwell was known for his left-wing views, but refused to throw his lot in with any political party.

- Orwell believed that power corrupted people. He wrote *Animal Farm*, which is a political fable, to show this. This is why all the idealism at the beginning comes to nothing; as soon as the animals seize power, the rot sets in.

- There were no other texts similar to *Animal Farm* at the time. In fact, many publishers wrongly thought it was a children's book because it had animals in it. A shocked Orwell went round bookshops when the book was published, removing copies from the children's section and placing them on more suitable shelves!

As you can see, just a brief look at the background helps you understand the book better. You aren't expected to do reams of research about this yourself, but just tune in to what you're told. So do listen when your English teacher witters on about the life and times of your set text author – it might come in very useful.

How do I write right in English?

Which of the following will get you a good grade in your Eng Lit exam? Choose the ones which are bound to make the examiners give you tick after tick.

- ✔ A sparkling personality.
- ✔ A good understanding of your set texts.
- ✔ The way you flick your fringe back.
- ✔ Knowing what pathetic fallacy is.
- ✔ How nice you are to your mates.
- ✔ Having a file of detailed notes on your set texts.
- ✔ Your dead posh trainers.
- ✔ Having seen a performance of the play you're studying.
- ✔ The fact you really want a high grade.
- ✔ The fact you've enjoyed your set texts immensely.

Answer: None of them. They are useless, the file of notes, the understanding of technical jargon, your grasp of the central issues, your expensive trainers – *unless you let the examiner know you've got them* (not the trainers).

And how do you do that? By what you write, and the way you write. That's why this section is essential reading.

You mean I needn't have ploughed my way through the other sections? Now you tell me!

Not at all. The earlier sections tell you what to write – now we're going to look at how to write it.

I have some good ideas, but sometimes I struggle to find the words for them.

When my essays come back to me, the teacher's scribbled 'expression!' all over it but I don't get what she means.

My essays are always too short.

There are *five* different kinds of writing tasks you may be asked to do. Each of them requires a slightly different approach, although they all have elements in common too. To help guide you through this section, each kind of writing will have an icon to represent it. These icons will show whether the part of this section you are reading applies to the kind of writing you want to check out:

 In coursework essay writing you have plenty of time for research, planning and developing your ideas.

 In timed essays in an exam you have to get as much down as quickly as you can, and you have to learn to be *selective* (homing in on the right details to get your point across).

 In empathetic and creative writing, whether you are pretending to be a character in a text, or writing a story inspired by the text, even though you're constructing an original piece of writing, you have to link yourself to the text in several ways.

 In comparing and contrasting, you have to cover a range of texts and look at them both or all together (often comparing and contrasting poems or a film version of a text and the text itself).

 In answering questions on a poem or passage you must explore detail.

Otherwise, they all have a lot in common, as you will see.

Stage one – focussing on the question

Understanding exactly what you have to do in any writing task is vital. So the first thing you must always do is READ THE QUESTION. Then read the question again. And just when you think it's safe to come out of the water, read the question again. Examine each word. Check you've seen everything in the question, and that whatever you're going to go on to write addresses all parts of the question. And just remember – exam nerves can stop you reading questions properly. So, in exams, it's doubly important to make sure you've understood exactly what you're being asked.

 Some examining boards give you a list of bulleted points under the essay title to help you structure your answer. Use them. Check you write something to cover each bullet point.

As brilliant as this guide is, we can't cover all the possible questions you'll be asked. We can, however, give you some sample question wordings to look at.

1. How important is (a character, a scene, etc.) to the text?

Don't just describe the character or scene but make sure you explain how it connects to the whole of the text and what it tells you about the text – that's its importance.

2. How does (a character or scene) *contribute* to the text?

Tackle this by firstly describing the character or scene, then relate it to the text as a whole. Say what the character or scene tells you about the themes in the text.

3. How does a writer *present his or her ideas* in a text?

Usually through character or action or setting or plot. Write about as many of those as seems sensible. Say what the main ideas in the text are in the beginning of your essay.

4. How does a writer *present a character or setting* in a text?

This question directs you to the writer's technique. The answer will be something like, through description of the character, through what the character says, the diction used to describe the setting, etc.

5. Why does a character do the things they do? (E.g. Why does Macbeth kill Duncan?)

Look at all the influences on the character, the character himself, things outside the character that he cannot control.

6. How far would you consider a character to be to blame for something?

The answer is either *totally*, or *up to a point*, or *hardly*, or *not at all*. Your writing should argue your opinions by proving them with detailed reference to the text.

> **TOP TIP**
> Practise looking at old exam papers and studying the wording of the questions. Decide what you think the examiner is really looking for. The more familiar you are with the way questions are phrased, the happier you'll feel on exam day.

137

OK. So you've read and re-read the question or task set. You've got a pretty good idea of what the examiner is asking you. Now try to answer the question in just one sentence.

Now you're talking! I always thought short essays were best. I mean, why bore the examiner? Surely he needs a life too. And—

I think you've jumped the gun here. Answering a question in just one sentence is only the start. It helps you develop a clear overview of the territory you're going to cover, and acts as a double check that you're answering the question properly.

For example:

How does George Orwell present his ideas about the corruption of power in *Animal Farm*?

Could be answered by saying:

He presents the corruption of power through the story of how the pigs take over and fight among themselves, by the way the slogans the animals chant are gradually altered, by the end of the novel where the pigs are indistinguishable from men, by the

change in atmosphere from the joy at the beginning of the revolution through to the misery at the end, in particular, Boxer's betrayal.

That's quite a long sentence.

Yes, but it answers the question and provides the beginning of an essay plan, if you write a little under each section.

I don't see why you need to do that. I reckon just about everything in Animal Farm is basically Orwell presenting his ideas about the corruption of power, so I could just tell the story of the novel, which is a lot easier.

139

And a lot less likely to get you a good grade. That's because you wouldn't be answering a question so much as repeating the contents of the text in your own words, a fairly pointless activity. For example:

Irrelevant answers are boring too. Not only that, by cramming your answers with stuff that won't win you marks, you're leaving no room for the stuff that *will* get you marks. Be warned.

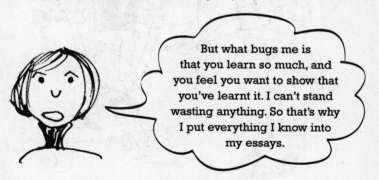

And that's why you aren't getting the best marks.

If you were going out for the night, you wouldn't wear your whole wardrobe just because you bought all those clothes – you'd only wear your best gear. It's the same with essays.

Stage two – brainstorming and researching

OK. I've answered the question set in one sentence like you said. And now I'm ready to write.

Oh no, you're not.

Oh yes, I am.

This isn't a pantomime.

Oh yes, it is.

I shall ignore that. The next stage for any serious GCSE Lit candidate is researching or brainstorming. They provide the magic ingredient for a first-class piece of writing.

143

Researching

 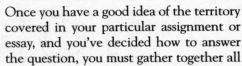 Once you have a good idea of the territory covered in your particular assignment or essay, and you've decided how to answer the question, you must gather together all the information which will help you to make your points. Without proof, even your most brilliant, ground-breaking ideas are almost worthless.

Doing coursework means you have the time to search for the best evidence.

You might look in:

- Your notes.
- Your copy of the text with its annotations.

Flick through these, skim reading, to see what quotations, incidents, or descriptions help you back up your points, and make a list of them in an easy-to-find, accessible way.

For example, if you're working on *To Kill a Mockingbird*, and you want to prove Atticus is a good father, you might jot down...

> He is willing to compromise with his children. (He allows Scout to carry on reading at home if she agrees to go to school.)
>
> He has firm standards for his children. (He tells Jem off for mimicking the neighbours in his play.)
>
> He evidently loves his children. (He calls Scout "baby".)

There are many other points, but this is what coursework essay notes should look like. With all this on paper, writing your essay should be a walkover.

Many students are tempted to skip the research stage. Here are some things to do while researching that might help to take away those I've-got-to-write-a-GCSE-Literature-essay blues.

1. Consume a whole packet of mints.
2. Trim your fingernails with your teeth.
3. Push your hair back so it doesn't fall in your face.
4. Play some non-distracting music in the background – heavy metal not recommended.
5. Reward yourself at the end of your research with a treat – a phone call to a friend, a session in front of the TV.

Patience counts for as much in essay writing as natural brilliance. Careful research always pays dividends. What separates the successes from the failures is the amount of time you're prepared to put in.

> **No. I don't believe that. The people in my class who do well don't work that hard.**

So they say. Do you believe everything your mates tell you?

> Well, no, but… Now, listen.
> I've thought of an objection. In exams
> you don't have the time to research. In
> our board's syllabus we only have half
> an hour to write an essay – surely I've
> got to spend all the time writing?

Brainstorming

In an exam, brainstorming takes the place of research.
You spend a few moments gathering your thoughts
together and thinking speedily through your set
texts, jotting down evidence that will help you argue.

You could arrange your ideas in a spider diagram:

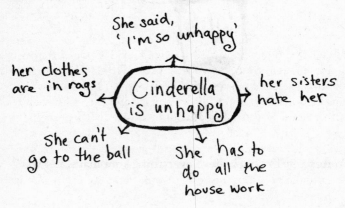

She said,
'I'm so unhappy'

her clothes
are in rags

Cinderella
is unhappy

her sisters
hate her

She can't
go to the ball

She has to
do all the
house work

I shall ignore that. Around the legs of your spider you can jot down evidence.

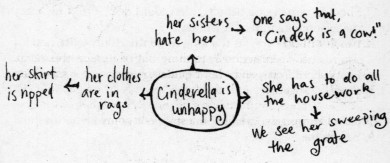

This way you have something to guide you as you write the essay.

Try brainstorming for ideas now. Think of your favourite album or piece of music. Write it in a circle and think of as many reasons you like it as possible. Then extend the leg of each reason with evidence – a snatch of your favourite lyrics, perhaps?

Q. How long should I spend planning an essay in an exam?

A. Approximately one-tenth of the time you have to write it. For example, a 30-minute essay would need around three to five minutes good quality thinking time.

Q. Where should I write my plan?

A. On a loose sheet of paper so it's still in front of you as you turn over your answer book. Wasteful, but efficient.

Q. What if I decide halfway through my essay that my plan is wrong? Do I abandon it?

A. A tricky one. Ask yourself first of all if you're not just feeling nervous and lacking in confidence. If you're sure it's not that, write a "hinge" in your essay explaining your change of thinking. Example of a "hinge":

Although it seems from the evidence given above that Macbeth is a hero, we see later in the play how his character rapidly deteriorates.

Q. Should I write out a detailed plan so if I don't finish my essay the examiner can read my notes?

A. No. It will take you far too long to do this. Only write notes if you realize you're seriously running out of time in the exam. Plans should only ever be a guide for you, not a substitute essay.

Q. How can I get an indelible ink stain out of my favourite shirt?

A. Search me.

Q. Well, you seem to know the answer to everything else...

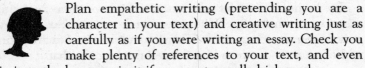

Plan empathetic writing (pretending you are a character in your text) and creative writing just as carefully as if you were writing an essay. Check you make plenty of references to your text, and even imitate the language in it if you want a really high mark.

Research and brainstorming for comparison work is vitally important. Try to arrange your plan in two columns:

<u>The Lady of Shalott</u>   <u>Porphyria's Lover</u>

weather is calm   weather is stormy
told from her point of view   told from his point of view
she knows she will die   she's murdered suddenly

both women look
beautiful at the end

Stage three – planning and organization

 You know the feeling. You're sitting comfortably watching TV, legs over the side of the settee, and your favourite soap begins from the cliff-hanging moment it finished at yesterday. Then there's a shout – or rather a demented scream – from upstairs…

"TIDY YOUR ROOM!!!"

When you get to your bedroom you can see that your parent was justified. It's a tip. Your bin is full to overflowing and stray underwear decorates the floor. Someone – you? – has been leafing through your magazines and scattered them everywhere. What is your deodorant doing on the bookshelves, and why is there a can of lemonade under your bed? Your trainers are under the desk along with your geography notes and three letters from your pen-friend.

So you start to sort it all out. Rubbish in the bin, clothes in the wardrobe, schoolbooks on the desk. After a while you get quite carried away and can't quite believe that this new, spacious bedroom is yours. You get a tremendous feeling of satisfaction from looking at your tidy, organized room. Knowing where everything is makes you feel in control...

As if.

But the same applies to planning your lit essays. After you've brainstormed or researched, you'll have a mass of notes, or lists of important pages of quotations in front of you. All this will help you write your essay. But your notes are all over the place. If you skimmed through your text, you might have been collecting points on different topics as you went through. Your heart sinks as you try to make sense of it all.

Don't despair. Run along to the nearest stationery shop and buy yourself a new set of highlighters and coloured pencils. Read through the notes you've just made and colour-code them so notes that relate to the same major point are all the same colour. Organize and sort your notes so that you can see your way clearly through them. Remember, knowing where everything is makes you feel in control.

Look at this example of notes that have been sorted.

How Does Steinbeck Present Lenny in 'Of Mice and Men'?

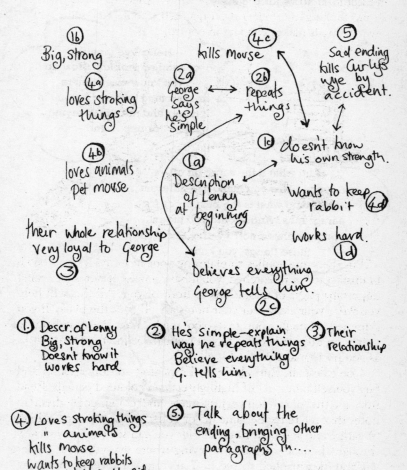

(1b) Big, strong

(4a) loves stroking things

(4b) loves animals Pet mouse

(4c) kills mouse

(2a) George says he's simple ↔ (2b) repeats things

(5) Sad ending kills Curlys wye by accident.

(1c) doesn't know his own strength.

(1a) Description of Lenny at beginning

their whole relationship very loyal to George (3)

Wants to keep rabbit (4d)

works hard. (1d)

Believes everything George tells him. (2c)

① Descr. of Lenny
Big, strong
Doesn't know it
works hard

② He's simple—explain way he repeats things Believe everything G. tells him.

③ Their relationship

④ Loves stroking things
" animals
kills mouse
wants to keep rabbits
– shows his gentle side.

⑤ Talk about the ending, bringing other paragraphs in....

Here the number system helps the writer to see how many major paragraphs there'll be in the final essay. Then the writer sorted the paragraphs out and put them in a logical order. This provides a clear framework for the essay.

Hello. I've thought of another problem. How do you know when you're researching whether a point is minor and not worth saying, or important?

And what if the same bit of evidence helps you make two different points? And what is the best order for paragraphs? And should you indent paragraphs or not? I worry about these things, you know.

Quite. I'm pleased to see it. You've raised several important issues here.

1. Picking the right evidence

Common sense should help you decide whether a point is substantial or trivial. At the same time, try to have a balance in your essay between small details that back you up, and wider, more general points that might relate to the whole text.

> **Goldilocks is greedy. This is supported by the fact she eats three bowls of porridge [wider, more general point] and the blissful look on her face as she finishes the last one [smaller detail].**

In fact, you should try to be selective (choose detail well) AND wide-ranging (picking evidence from all over the text).

Aw, come on! You're contradicting yourself. You're saying I've got to pick evidence from everywhere but keep it relevant!

That isn't actually a contradiction. It's especially important if you're answering a question based on an extract from your text. You'll be expected to work in considerable detail looking at language, etc., but also you'll have to hint pretty heavily that you know more, by linking details in the passage with related details in the rest of the text.

153

So how do you do that?

OK. Say I asked you to describe your living room, but you wanted to show me you knew the rest of your house too. You might say...

> In our living room we have a paisley settee which contrasts with the tartan wallpaper. This Scottish theme is continued in the kitchen where there is a collection of miniature malt whisky bottles on the shelf. We have a coal-effect gas fire in front of the settee which is always on as the rest of the house does not have central heating. Near the French windows leading to our small garden is a turquoise table with four chairs around it, including one bright yellow one that used to be in the master bedroom but was brought downstairs when it was replaced with a psychedelic easy chair..."

Here the writer is both answering the question and hinting that he knows more. Write your lit essays like this and you won't go far wrong.

2. Reusing evidence

If one quotation or incident supports several points, you can use it several times. The second or third time just refer to it briefly, and try to back it up with other, similar evidence...

> Right from the beginning of Macbeth we can see that the witches are a force of evil. They say "Fair is foul, and foul is fair" which means that to them evil is a good thing.

(A page later…)

> Once Macbeth is King we feel that evil rules, and it is true to say "Fair is foul, and foul is fair". Many other characters call him a tyrant.

(A page later…)

> **In conclusion, we can see how easy it is for wickedness to conquer goodness, and sometimes how little divides them, so "Fair is foul, and foul is fair."**

Try never to use a quotation more than three times in an essay. Three times is the absolute max – twice is preferable.

3. Ordering paragraphs

There's a golden rule about the best order for paragraphs in essays… **Save the best till last.**

Begin an essay low-key, with the more everyday paragraphs first. Make the usual points. Then build up to a crescendo so the most important stuff and your best ideas are at the end – your finale with fireworks. Leave the person who reads your essay seriously impressed with you. End with a bang, not a whimper. Remember, what's read last will stay in the examiner's head the longest … the longest.

Try also to make your paragraphs progress logically. Place connected paragraphs next to each other. Make sure each paragraph is linked to the ones before and after it with an explanatory sentence.

> **…As we can see, Eddie's feelings for Catherine are rather more than those of a father-figure for a daughter. Catherine's relationship with Bea is more conventional.**

155

> **Bea is Catherine's aunt, and seems extremely fond of her. They spend a lot of time...**

Linking paragraphs like this is vital. It helps the reader (or marker) of your essay to follow your train of thought. And if they can't follow your train of thought, then they'll get derailed, and your marks will suffer.

4. Indenting paragraphs

It's always vital to indent paragraphs. If you don't, the examiner might think you're not using paragraphs. Not writing in paragraphs is bad news. Examiners consider them to be the essential building blocks of an essay.

By now you've absorbed the question, researched or brainstormed, organized your material into paragraphs, decided on the order of the paragraphs ... and you're off. You're ready to start writing. Or are you? There's just the small matter of the introduction.

Stage four – the introduction

"Hello! This is the Jubilee Introduction Agency calling! I'm just ringing to let you know about a new gentleman who's just been put on our books...

"...A Scottish gentleman.
Tall, dark, aged around 35. His interests
include fighting, feasting and the supernatural.
He's very ambitious – says he wants
to be king one day...
...He's looking for a lady in her twenties who'll
spur him on a bit, and so I thought of you..."
Is that the kind of introduction
you mean?

Very funny. Although an introduction in an essay does perform a similar function – it introduces the reader to your essay and indicates how the essay's going to develop.

In all forms of introduction, the trick is to ask yourself what the *reader* needs to know before he or she begins to read your essay. As the writer, it's your job to be crystal clear. As someone who wants the highest grade possible, it's also your job to prove to the examiner you're answering the question absolutely relevantly. So always mention the question.

157

An introduction should be around three sentences. It should put the question you're answering into your own words. It provides a link to the first paragraph. (Really stylish introductions can even begin with quotations.)

Why does Harper Lee choose to tell *To Kill a Mockingbird* from Scout's viewpoint?

To Kill A Mockingbird is a novel about racism in the States in the 1930s. The events in the novel are told by Scout, a girl of eight years old. Many interesting effects are achieved by this viewpoint. We learn about racism through the eyes of a child and about Scout herself.
   At the beginning of the novel, Scout is not yet at school...

 An introduction might only be one sentence. It acknowledges the question and links to the first paragraph.

Scout is the eight-year-old narrator of *To Kill A Mockingbird*, and her viewpoint adds a great deal to the novel.
   We first meet Scout...

 An introduction will state what the two things are you're comparing, and mention their similarities. Then it will provide a link to the whole comparison essay.

Compare and contrast Tennyson's "The Lady Of Shalott" with Browning's "Porphyria's Lover".
Both "The Lady of Shalott" and "Porphyria's Lover" are pre-twentieth century poems in which a lady

dies through her love for a man. There the resemblance ends.

Tennyson's poem is set in the days of King Arthur...

WARNING

Never be tempted to put the conclusion in place of the introduction. It's your essay that answers the question, not the introduction. Don't give the game away too soon. Don't write...

> **Harper Lee chooses Scout as a narrator because as a child she needs things explained to her and she gets more upset about the events in Maycomb than an adult would. Also children are more interesting sometimes than adults...**

...as an *introduction*. That is your *conclusion*. Look again at the introduction on page 158 and see the difference. An introduction opens an essay up, a conclusion closes it down.

Stage five – start writing

With your introduction clear, relevant and tempting the reader on, you're ready to start writing the main part of your essay. You're sitting at a desk or table (beds are only for sleeping) with your text in front of you (not even you know it all by heart). Your notes and plan are in front of you too. You've turned off the TV – it took some discipline but, hey, you're cool. You nicked your kid sister's mints to help you concentrate, and you begin.

At last. Let it all pour out.

Pour out? You know you've got to think as you write, and especially think about how you express yourself. However good your ideas are, unless you find the right words to convey them, you're a non-starter.

If you stay with these dos and don'ts, you won't go far wrong.

DO use formal, everyday English.

DON'T use slang. Slang is as out of place in a literature essay as a leather-clad biker at the vicar's tea party. Not sure whether the word you want to use is slang or not? Try this simple test.

Slang words, when taken literally, make nonsense of your sentence. For example:

- *The book is brilliant* literally means *The book is shining with an almost blinding light*.

- *My boyfriend is really cool* literally means *My boyfriend's body temperature is lower than normal*.

Can you detect which of the following pairs of sentences contains a word used as slang?

160

1. a) I spent a total of five pounds.
   b) The album I bought is totally wonderful.

2. a) The colour you dyed your hair is wicked.
   b) Lady Macbeth is wicked.

3. a) Romeo and Juliet are both dead.
   b) The play, *Romeo and Juliet*, is dead good.

Answers on page 200.

Hold on a minute. You've been using slang throughout this book. Hypocrite.

True. But *The Alternative GCSE Guide to English Literature* is an informal book, so I can use informal language. Your literature essays are formal, so you must choose the correct language. In the same way, there are a number of abbreviations in this book (shouldn't, can't, etc, there's) but you must never use abbreviations in essays.

Not even if I'm running out of time?

Well, I suppose if you only have five minutes left...

DON'T use words that you don't understand. That might sound daft, but everyone is tempted from time to time to use a word they heard recently and sounds dead clever – maybe one your teacher used – but if you use it wrongly, you'll be a laughing stock. Don't raid the thesaurus for words. You might misapply those too. Stick with the words you know and love.

DO use appropriate literary terms. Chapter two on page 49 introduces you to plenty of those. Get into the habit of using them. Your writing will sound a lot more professional.

DON'T use vague words with wide meanings. "Nice" could be applied to a kind, thoughtful character in a text, but also the weather, the time you had at aunty Doris's, your dad's new tie – anything. So it's not a helpful word. Also avoid "caring", "good", "bad", etc.

DON'T repeat words or phrases.

Oh, come on! You mean I can only use words like "the", "and" and "but" once?

No, of course not. But a good essay never repeats significant words. This is one of the trickiest parts of essay writing and this book is going to help you with it.

You've found evidence for your point, and you write...

This shows that Piggy is despised by all the boys.

Fine: but you must now try to avoid the phrase "this shows that". Substitute instead...

This implies that...
This suggests that...
This tells us that...
The writer is persuading us that...
We can see from this that...
This conveys the impression that...

This makes us think that...
This confirms the idea that...
This denotes that...
This is evidence that...
This proves that...

Using that list and any other words or expressions that seem OK, see if you can rewrite the following mini-essay getting rid of the repetitions.

Goldilocks is a risk-taker. We know this because she enters the three bears' cottage. She is also curious. We know this because she tries each of the chairs. She is then tired. We know this because she lies down

on the beds. Then she is hungry. We know this because she eats the porridge. She is easily frightened. We know this because she runs out of the cottage when the three bears arrive home with air-rifles and machetes.

Here's a possible improved version – yours could be just as good, or better!

The fact Goldilocks is a risk-taker is implied by the way she enters the three bears' cottage. Later the writer reveals Goldilocks's curiosity when we see her test each of the chairs in turn. She tries the beds too; this could suggest that she is feeling tired. The way she eats from all the bowls of porridge is evidence that she is hungry. The fact she is easily frightened is proved without a shadow of doubt when she runs screaming from the cottage followed by three crazed bears wielding air-rifles and machetes.

Also be aware that you cannot repeat endlessly a key word in the title. If you are asked if Macbeth is ambitious or not, you'll have to find some words or phrases which mean the same, or almost the same, as ambitious. (For example, keen to reach the top, driven, highly motivated, desperate to be king.) This way you can avoid starting every sentence, "We know Macbeth is ambitious because…"

Just remember, using the same word or phrase over and over again can become monotonous.

Yes: using the same word or phrase over and over again can become monotonous.

Using the same word or phrase over and over again can become monotonous.

DO write in the first person. Use the word "we" as in, "We can see from the beginning of the novel that…" You can use "I" too, especially and importantly when you are asked a question about your own personal response.

Never use "you" as in, "You feel that it's bound to end in tears."

Some people like to write impersonally, e.g. "It can be seen that Shylock is mercenary." This can, however, get a little dull. Discuss with your teacher his or her stylistic preferences.

DON'T praise too much. You might think the examiner will love you if you claim you adore your set text, have never read a better book and want to marry it and have its babies, but your marker will not be impressed. English Literature GCSE is supposed to teach you critical skills. You sound naïve if you praise everything indiscriminately.

DO practise your writing skills frequently and take your teacher's advice if you're told you need to improve your style.

DO take trouble with spelling, presentation and grammar. Marks will be lost if you make lots of mistakes. If you have trouble with your spelling, make a point of learning off by heart the correct spellings of your set text authors and the names of important characters and settings.

I remember reading somewhere that Shakespeare spelt his name differently on different manuscripts...

Yes, but he didn't have to pass his GCSE English Literature.

Not fair, is it?

No, it's not. But spelling is important if you want to get great marks.

DO learn the rules for setting out titles, authors' names and quotations.

1. Titles
Always make *titles* stand out when you refer to them. You can

either use speech marks around them, underline them or use upper case letters throughout. This is especially important when the title of a text is the same as the name of one of the characters e.g. Macbeth or Jane Eyre.

Title =	"Macbeth" or <u>Macbeth</u> or MACBETH
Character =	Macbeth
Title =	"Jane Eyre" or <u>Jane Eyre</u> or JANE EYRE
Character =	Jane Eyre

2. Authors' names

Male authors can be referred to either by their full name or surname, for example, George Orwell or Orwell. Some people prefer female authors only to be referred to by their full names, for example, Jane Austen, Harper Lee, never Austen or Lee, though there is some disagreement about this. However, *never* refer to an author by their first name alone. Not unless you want to chat them up.

3. Quotations

Throughout your literature essay, you'll be referring to the text. Sometimes you'll be referring to an incident or moment without actually quoting the words in the text – this is called direct reference. You will not need to use quotation marks. Also get into the habit of referring to an incident briefly – never stray into telling the story. Try to avoid the clumsy phrase "the bit where..."

For example:

> **"Animal Farm" is sometimes humorous. For example, we smile when the pigs enter the farmhouse and take out some hams for burial.**

This is a good example of direct reference.

At other times, you will actually be using the words in the text. This is called direct quotation.

- Whenever you quote, use quotation marks. There is never any exception to this.

- Keep quotations brief. *You will get no credit for copying out chunks of the text.* Get into the habit of never quoting more than a couple of sentences or a couple of lines of a poem. An effective quotation is usually 10-12 words, no more.

- Call a quotation a quotation. It's not a "quote". The word "quote" is a verb (I quote, you quote, he/she/it/Jack/Jill quotes). The noun is "quotation". Using the word "quote" instead is incorrect and will irritate your examiner. Irritating an examiner is never a good idea...

- When you are quoting more than one line of verse or poetry, set it out in the middle of your writing like this:

   Lewis Carroll's "Jabberwocky" starts with a description of the setting of his nonsense poem.
   "Twas brillig, and the slithy toves
   Did gyre and gimble in the wabe."
   We do not know what these words mean, and the effect is humorous.

- When you are quoting words from a poem that begin on one line and end on the next, use a slash to show where one line ends and the new one begins:

   Lewis Carroll informs us that "the slithy toves/Did gyre and gimble." We form the impression that some small animals are playing friskily.

- You don't need to underline quotations *or* give a page or act and scene reference, or write them in different coloured ink.

- Try to make your quotations fit your own sentence. Never let

them hang loose without an explanation.
Don't write...

"Four legs good, two legs bad". The animals in the novel make up slogans to express their views.

Do write...

The animals in the novel make up slogans such as "Four legs good, two legs bad" to express their views.

- Don't use too many quotations in an essay. Leave room for your own explanations and response too!

All quotations must have quotation marks around them otherwise the examiner will think you're cheating by pretending the author's words are yours.

A difficulty arises if you are using your class notes to write an essay, and you've written down something your teacher said in class because it was devastatingly clever. Can you pass off your teacher's words as your own?

Perhaps. Only beware. If everyone in your class wrote the same thing down, the examiner will be faced with 20 identical phrases. Your own words are generally preferable – at least they're original.

Practise using your own words now by restating the following:

1. **Lady Macbeth is ruthlessly ambitious.**
2. **Atticus Finch is a modest, unassuming lawyer.**
3. **Napoleon is exploitative and power-hungry.**
4. **The beautiful lyricism of "The Lady of Shalott" contrasts with the dark tragedy of the narrative.**

Answers on page 200.

Stage Six – The Conclusion

All good things come to an end. Essays, too, have to be wound up, and writing a conclusion is the way to do it.

  A conclusion should sum up the answer to the question and best of all, make a rounding-off statement.

For example:

> **Question: What led to the tragedy of Romeo and Juliet?**
>
> **Your conclusion might be: Blame for the tragedy seems to be evenly spread. The families were at fault for continuing their feud, the lovers married too quickly and Friar Lawrence gave bad advice. Perhaps the play is more of a tragedy because no one is fully to blame. That is why *Romeo and Juliet* is such a great play.**

Conclusions for coursework should be two or three sentences, while conclusions for timed essays should be one or two sentences.

 Conclusions in comparison essays need to be slightly longer because you are pulling together two texts. Be prepared to write about half a page. Also see page 172 where more help is given with comparison essays.

Each of the five types of writing has other special considerations. Here are some of them.

1. Coursework
You might have the opportunity to get the teacher to look at your plans or a first draft of your essay. Teachers are not allowed to write your coursework for you –

Shame!

– but can help you to see where you might be going wrong, and suggest general improvements. If a teacher gives you advice, take it. Maybe your teacher's fashion sense leaves a lot to be desired, his jokes are older than the Flood and he's always leaving his copy of the set text in the staff room, but his advice on coursework is totally sound.

Don't get too carried away with the presentation of your coursework. Neatness and legibility are vital, true, but you won't get any more marks for state-of-the-art plastic folders, gold-plated ink or drenching your assignment in Armani after-shave.

2. Timed essays
See the next chapter on page 178.

3. Empathetic and creative writing
Empathetic writing is where you pretend to be a character in your set text. If you have to do this:

● Re-tell incidents in the text from the point of view of your character.

- Stay in character – don't revert to yourself.

- Try to use the same kind of language that the character uses.

- Interpret events from the character's standpoint. Although Macbeth is the villain, if you were Lady Macbeth you'd see him as someone who could be the hero, but failed because he was too weak.

Still plan your writing, and still try to use an occasional quotation. Just pretend you are impersonating your character, and you won't go far wrong.

If you have a creative piece to write, be guided by the title you're given, but don't be tempted to stray too far from the text. Never miss out on an opportunity to strut your stuff in front of the examiner.

4. Compare and contrast

Oh, good. I'm pleased you're going to talk about this. Everyone taking GCSE has to be able to compare and contrast something.

True.

And what I can never suss out,
is if you're comparing two poems, right,
or even three or four poems, do you write
about each one in turn, or do you mix
them all up and write about them all
together. Like, what are the rules?

There are no rules as such, but an easy way of comparing and contrasting is as follows:

- Write your introduction saying how the texts, or versions of the text, are similar, but different.

- Answer the question set about the first poem or text.

- Answer the question set about the second poem or text, but every so often refer very briefly to the first poem or text.

- Continue doing this with the third and subsequent texts.

- If a thought occurs to you that links two texts, *include it*. You're bound to get credit for it.

- Write a slightly longer conclusion in which you bring together all the main similarities and differences between the texts you're comparing.

5. Answering questions on a passage
There's little planning involved here. You just need to remember two golden rules.

- Answer in as much detail as possible, looking at how the writer writes.

- Remember to make an occasional reference to the rest of the text.

And now ... exclusively to *GCSE English Literature* we take you behind the scenes at an essay rehearsal. Read on to see how this young, wannabe essay is coached up to Oscar-winning standard...
But first, the text.

> Stop all the clocks, cut off the telephone,
> Prevent the dog from barking with a juicy bone,
> Silence the pianos and with muffled drum
> Bring out the coffin, let the mourners come.
>
> Let aeroplanes circle moaning overhead
> Scribbling on the sky the message He is Dead,
> Put crepe bows round the white necks of the public
>   doves,
> Let the traffic policemen wear black cotton gloves.
> He was my North, my South, my East and West,
> My working week and my Sunday rest,
> My noon, my midnight, my talk, my song;
> I thought that love would last forever: I was wrong.
>
> The stars are not wanted now: put out every one;
> Pack up the moon and dismantle the sun;
> Pour away the ocean and sweep up the wood.
> For nothing now can ever come to any good.
>
> W H Auden

Director: OK. I want you to write a paragraph on this poem from your GCSE anthology describing how it expresses feelings of bereavement. Just relax and take it easy. We know you're feeling nervous.

Young Essay: (*clears throat and ascends stage*) I think I'm ready now.

> *This poem by W H Auden is famous because it was used in* Four Weddings and a Funeral, *a film with Hugh Grant in it. Obviously this poem wasn't used in the weddings – joke! In this poem it says, "Stop all the clocks, cut off the telephone, / Prevent the dog from barking with a juicy bone, / Silence the pianos and with muffled drum / Bring out the coffin, let the mourners come. / Let aeroplanes circle—"*

Director: Cut! Cut! Do you call that an essay? I asked you to write about feelings of bereavement – not the modern cinema! Be relevant. And I'm not interested in your puerile jokes! And what do you mean by just repeating the poem? What does that tell me? I want to learn something. I want to be moved by your essay. Heaven give me strength!

Young Essay: I'm sorry, I really am, I'm really sorry, honest. Give me another chance, please!

Director: I shouldn't be doing this, but your father does own the theatre. OK. Now this time make some basic points about Auden's feelings and illustrate them from the text. Think – how does he feel?

175

Young Essay: *(takes deep breath)*

> *Auden feels very bad about the death of his friend because he doesn't want life to go on as normal. It says, "Stop all the clocks, cut off the telephone." He is so upset he thinks the whole world will be upset too which is why he wants aeroplanes to sky-write "He is Dead" and wants the policemen to be in mourning. Auden said his friend was everything to him, "my North, my South, my East and West". He is so sad he wants the world to come to an end because he doesn't need the stars and moon and oceans and wood any more. So I can conclude he is very upset indeed.*

(Ripple of applause from people in theatre.)

Director: Hmm. That's better. That's considerably better. You're answering the question, and you've even given evidence. I think we can make something of you yet. But wait. I have some ideas. Next time focus on the language Auden uses. Think about *how* he expresses himself, and what effects different words and phrases have. And while you're at it, use better words yourself. True, Auden is sad and upset. But you'd be sad and upset if your team lost or dinner was burnt. Put a bit of passion into it. Make your own writing reflect the intensity of feeling Auden experiences.

Young Essay: I don't know if I can. But I'll try. I've dreamed of this moment, writing an essay in front of you. Well, here goes.

> *Auden's poem begins with an order – "Stop all the clocks". This sudden command shocks us and makes us wonder what event has caused this. It is not until the last line of the first stanza that we learn someone has died; the words "coffin" and "mourners" introduce the subject of the poem. The regular rhyme and rhythm of the verse conveys the feeling of a funeral procession.*
>   *In the second stanza the range of the poem is widened; aeroplanes "moan'" – an onomatopoeic word – birds and traffic policemen are told to wear mourning. We begin to think someone very important has*

176

died. However, in the third stanza we see it is only someone important to the poet, someone who was "my North, my South, my East and West", someone who was in fact his whole world. He filled every day, every moment of every day for the poet. When Auden calls his dead friend his "song", this implies the joy he got from his presence in his life. The bitterness in the final line of the third stanza – "I thought that love would last for ever: I was wrong" – is chilling. Auden suggests that death is stronger than love. He feels not just sadness, but angry despair, and a sense of total devastation. In the fourth—

Director: Bravo! Bravo! Bravo! Bravissimo! This is wonderful. You've commented on language, expressed his feelings in your own words, and you've taken yourself inside the poet's head. I tell you. I'm moved. I am. (*Takes out his handkerchief and sobs.*)

Young Essay: Thank you, thank you so much. I couldn't have done it without you. I'll remember now to focus on language as well as make points. Can I have a Hollywood contract? Can I get to star in a film with Hugh Grant? I've always fancied Hugh Grant. I loved *Four Weddings and a Funeral…*

This is literally the worst exam!

The grand finale of the two years you spend studying English Literature at GCSE is your English Literature examination. This will be from two to two-and-a-half hours long. As with any exam, the key to success lies in preparation.

Preparing for your literature exam

At the moment most GCSE boards allow you to take copies of your set texts in with you; not all do, however. Either way, you're expected to know your set texts reasonably well.

How well? I mean, if I can take the books in with me, surely I don't have to do much revision?

You know what I'm going to say, don't you?

That I still have to revise?

Correct.

Yes, but not as much as other subjects like History and Chemistry where you have all those facts to learn?

Just as much, only you'll probably go about your revision in a slightly different way.

179

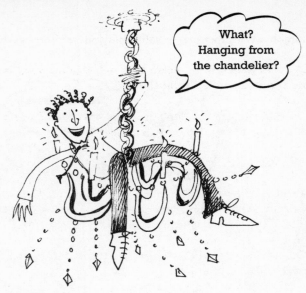

Original, certainly.

Here's another chance to win the jackpot with your revision skills as we begin the All-Star Revision Quiz. Make sure you have your fingers on the buzzers, and remember that your second wrong answer means you drop out from the quiz. With each correct answer your money doubles. Good luck, contestants!

– David… *When* do you do your English Literature revision?

– **Um – in the bath – I mean, Michael, I go over the stories of my set texts while I'm in the bath.**

– Good. As long as you don't drop your texts in the water. Lisa… How long do you revise for at a time?

– **Oh, four hours at a stretch, Michael.**

– Wrong answer. After an hour of revising everyone needs a short break otherwise your concentration is impaired. Jenny… How do you check you've remembered your set text?

– **I tell the story to the cat, Michael. Or if she's asleep, I make brief notes.**

– Good, correct answer. Saying things you've learned aloud is just as good as testing yourself by writing. Making notes is a good idea as you can look them over the night before the exam. And now, David… Who is with you when you revise?

– **Oh, right. My mates, I get them round. And I watch videos of great sporting moments. And my dad pops in from time to time with a cup of tea.**

– Sorry, wrong answer. Effective learning is best done alone although the occasional revision session with friends can help you with the difficult parts of texts. Lisa… How long does it take you to revise a set text?

– **Er, about three weeks because I do a little every day.**

– Excellent answer. Jenny… How many times do you read your set texts before the exam?

181

– Once? No – ten times. No – 50? I'm sorry, Michael...

– The right answer is at least three times. You read it by yourself, you study it in class, and then revise it. David... How do you visualize your set plays and novels?

– **I watch the videos. It's much easier than reading the texts. Why bother with the text?**

– Wrong! Watching videos is no substitute for studying the text. I'm sorry, David, but we'll have to lose you. Films can be quite different from the actual texts. Now. Lisa. Do you learn notes as well as your texts?

– **Not off by heart, no. But I look through them to help me understand the texts and see what the main themes are, or to remind myself what the characters are like.**

– Good. And Jenny – to equalise... At what time of day do you revise your set texts?

182

— **Late at night, after my other revision.**

— Jenny – I'm sorry – late at night means you'll fall asleep, get little done and have bad, Shakespeare-infested dreams. It's as important to learn your set texts as it is to learn the facts of any other subject.

   And so – Lisa – you have £200, but you can double it to £400 if you can answer the All-Star Challenge question. Will you take the challenge or go home with your £200?

— **I think I'll take the challenge, Michael.**

— Your set play is *Macbeth*, I believe, so your three-part question will come from that text. Lights down... Lisa... Who was the King of Scotland before Macbeth?

— **Duncan**.

— How did Macbeth murder Duncan?

— **He got the chamberlains – no – with a dagger – he killed him with a dagger. There was blood everywhere.**

— Correct. And for £400 ... what was the make of the dagger?

— **"Is this a dagger which I see before me, the handle toward my hand?" Yes – it is – but I can't read the manufacturer's name – it's on the other side. "Come, let me clutch thee! I have thee not..." Er, does it come from B & Q?**

— Oh, Lisa, Lisa, I'm so sorry. You were so nearly there. So very nearly there. But you lost – and we get to keep all our money for next week!

Revising for an open book examination

If you can take your texts in with you, obviously you needn't learn quotations off by heart, or memorize the detail of the text with almost perfect recall. You will, however, still need to know your texts quite thoroughly.

There are as many effective ways of revising as there are students. Check out with your mates how they learn their texts, especially those of your mates who seem to do well at literature. They won't mind dishing out their secrets – and if they do mind, then they're not worth having as mates.

Generally, you should be able to know the stories of your set texts AND know what points to make about characters, setting, plot, themes, writers' methods, etc. You should think as you revise – English Literature GCSE is more than just a memory test. On the other hand, the exam will be loads easier if you know your stuff.

If you don't believe that, try this simple test.

1. Describe what you had for dinner yesterday.

2. Describe what the Prime Minister had for dinner yesterday.

Question **1.** was easy. Because you were completely familiar with your meal the question didn't stress you out at all. Question **2.** (unless you are the Prime Minister or a close relation) was impossible – you didn't know your stuff.

Annotating texts

It's a good idea to know the rules about annotating texts for use in the exam.

Most boards say you're not allowed to write whole essays in the margins of your texts, and they wouldn't be very useful anyway. Your notes should be brief, explaining the odd word, underlining a key phrase or sentence, pointing out a literary device and jotting down its effect.

If you try to jam too much on to a page, you won't be able to make head nor tail of it in an exam. Use coloured pencils and different kinds of underlining so you can code your notes. Be organized.

Get to know where useful quotations and incidents are in your texts. Check with your teacher whether you're allowed Post-It notes, or whether you can turn down the corners of your pages. Practise flicking through your copy of the text to find key passages.

And most important of all – make sure you don't leave your copies of the texts at home on the big day!

Learning texts

Some of you will have to learn your set texts, including quotations. Don't feel hard done by – some people think it's actually easier to write well in a literature exam when you're not wasting time flicking through the text in a desperate attempt to find a passage that doesn't seem to exist any more.

Tips For Learning Quotations

- Keep quotations short.

- Write them out on Post-It notes and decorate your bedroom with them.

185

- Repeat them to yourself whenever you have a spare moment.

- Use them as chat-up lines – "How now, you secret, black and midnight hags!"

- Anything that rhymes is easier to learn than something that doesn't.

- Learn the spellings of the quotations too – practise writing them out.

- Make a poster of key quotations and stick it up on the back of the bathroom door.

But what if I have a good memory anyway and I think I can remember enough stuff from lessons to answer the questions in the exam?

A fatal error. In the examination situation, you're understandably nervous. Your left eyelid twitches, you try to stop your foot tapping beneath the desk. You read the question, and then your mind goes blank. If you've revised thoroughly, your mind will fill up again with relevant facts and information. If you haven't revised thoroughly, your mind will stay blank, utterly, utterly blank...

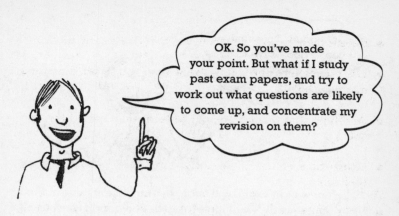

OK. So you've made your point. But what if I study past exam papers, and try to work out what questions are likely to come up, and concentrate my revision on them?

Listen carefully and repeat after me... **There is no foolproof method for guessing the questions that will come up.**

In fact, there can be a serious disadvantage in preparing set topics hoping they will come up. If the topic does come up, you're likely to be so thrilled you don't read the question properly and pour out everything you know when it hasn't been asked for. You're better off practising your skills and expecting the unexpected.

So there's no point in looking at past papers?

I didn't say that. In fact, an essential part of your preparation should be looking at past papers and familiarizing yourself with the kind of wording your board uses. You'll usually do this in class.

187

Oh good. Does that mean I don't have to do old questions?

As if. Before your lit exam, you *must* practise writing to time. Find out how long roughly you'll have for each essay, and give yourself a trial run. That way you find out what half an hour feels like, and you see how much it's possible to get down in that time.

The Bad News
There won't be time to write down everything you know about your set texts – so you must be selective.

The Good News
Half an hour goes really quickly when you're having fun...

THE MOST COMMON MISTAKES MADE BY CANDIDATES IN ENG LIT EXAMS

- Not reading the questions properly.
- Mis-spelling authors' and characters' names.
- Spending too long on the introduction and then running out of time.
- Being tempted into telling the story of the text rather than answering the question.
- Forgetting it was Eng Lit that day and revising Biology instead the night before.

As with any GCSE, you must aim. . .
- to learn effectively – choose a quiet room and have a short break after you've worked for about an hour.
- to go to bed early the night before the exam.
- to take a few deep breaths before the exam to relax those shoulder muscles.
- to make sure your pen's not going to run out.

NEWS OF THE SUN

English Literature Uncovered!
An examiner spills the beans, and his coffee, as our intrepid interviewer's questions get more and more personal. The national dailies tried to scoop us, and offered vast sums of money for this no-holds-barred interview – but we weren't selling...

Is it true that examiners are repressed sadists who, having been severely traumatised as children, spend their adulthood inflicting pain on others?

No, no! In fact, the reverse is the case. Most of us enjoyed our education and that's why we've stayed in it. We're mainly teachers when we're not examining. In our leisure time we like to watch TV, go to the big match, travel and go out to eat! Sadists? I think not.

Hmm. I'm not convinced. Do you realize how you've made thousands upon thousands of innocent candidates suffer through devilishly worded questions?

Oh dear! My apologies. In fact, we all try to be as helpful as possible. That's why it's been the fashion in recent years to list bullet points under the questions, to tell candidates what we expect them to write about.

And do they?

Funny you should ask that.

Most of them do but some don't. I really can't understand why. I mean, we're handing it to them on a plate, so to speak. All they have to do is use each bullet point as a kind of sub-heading and write a paragraph or two under that. I know I would.

And another thing. Students suffer untold anxiety when they can't decide what question to choose. How do you know which question is the easiest before you're halfway through it?

Oh dear. We honestly thought students preferred choice. It gives them a chance to answer the question they think they can do best at. But I can see the dilemma. The best advice I can give is try some quick brainstorming – that will soon show you which question is going to be easier for you.

How do you mean?

Spend a minute or so thinking through what you would write for each question. It's likely you'll find more to say about one than the other. Answer the one where more ideas occur. If it's about equal, go for the one you find most interesting.

What do you wear when you're marking scripts?

A flowery pink negligee and two false... Excuse me! I don't see what this has got to do with it! Please restrict yourself to asking questions about the exam.

Sorry, guv. All right. Are there any other ways you try to help candidates?

Oh, yes. We print all the instructions for the exam clearly on the cover page. Sometimes we even tell you how to long to spend on each question. We know candidates are nervous and we recommend reading the cover sheet carefully. It stops you making silly mistakes, such as answering all the questions from Section A when the instructions say answer one question from Section A and one from Section B, and calms you down and gets you focussed. And another thing—

Go on. You're intent on proving you're the nice guy, aren't you?

Another thing. We always let the candidate know how many marks are allotted for each question. That helps them decide how much time to spend on each question. A question worth 50 marks obviously needs longer than a question only worth 20 marks. Putting the marks by the questions is our way of hinting what we want from candidates.

So let's recap. You're saying candidates should come in, read the instructions carefully, put some thought into deciding which question to answer, and then work out how much time they have for each question.

Absolutely. And then make a brief plan to help them to answer the question precisely.

But you don't say that anywhere on the paper!

It's common sense. If we ask a question, we expect a planned answer. Just like you do from me.

Don't get cheeky! I'm in the driving seat here. So let me get this straight. Are you saying there's no point writing anything unless you're answering the question set?

191

Yes. I suppose I am.

Do you realize that this means each candidate is going to have to spend three to five minutes thinking through their answer and jotting down a brief plan before they start writing?

Er, yes.

Pouring out everything you know is no good?

No good at all.

(So that's where I've been going wrong!) Ahem! Seeing as you're such a nice guy...

And remarkably good-looking.

...Yes, remarkably good-looking – you must be very generous on candidates with untidy handwriting, or those who make the odd spelling mistake.

Unfortunately, we're not. By law we have to give marks for accurate spelling, *punctuation and grammar. If your spelling's a disaster, you won't be awarded those marks. We won't penalize untidy handwriting if we can read it. Anything that's illegible is not worth the paper it's written on. And if your handwriting is difficult to decipher, we'll get irritated reading your script. And when I'm irritated...*

OK, OK, calm down. Is there anything else that's a turn-off for you?

Hmm. Let me see. My main gripe is reading essays that don't answer the question. But I've already said that. It annoys me when candidates draw all their evidence just from the beginning of the text. It annoys me when they call a play a "book". It annoys me when they say something like "this is a simile" and don't talk about its effect. I hate it when candidates make a statement about the text and don't give the evidence. Oh, and I can't stand inaccurate quotations.

And silly ideas about the set text.

No. At least if someone's trying to say something original they're moving in the right direction. Did you know, in English Literature exams we never deduct marks for wrong ideas? You just don't get any marks for them. So if in doubt, put it down. Your idea is either brilliant, in which case you'll get double marks, or daft, in which case I'll have a smile, and you won't lose anything.

What kind of books do you like reading?

Anything with cowboys in it. I love railway timetables too.

hee hee hee

TRAIN TIMES

And those lovely little poems

you get inside birthday cards! And Dennis the Menace. He's my hero. And Desperate Dan. And the Bash Street Kids.

Sorry I asked. Now tell me. What kind of examination answer really pleases you? What are the magic ingredients that make for a first class answer?

The three R's: Relevance, Reference to the text, and Response. If you answer the question stage by stage, prove your ideas with detail from the text and show you're involved with the text, you're a winner.

Ah! But what if you don't like the set texts. Not everyone does, you know.

True. A response doesn't mean that you have to like your texts. So many candidates think they have to gush about the texts, but that's not we want. Oh, no! Responding to a text really means trying to get below its

surface, interpreting it, saying what you think it means, and what the writer's getting at. Or you could even say how a text makes you feel. Or put it this way: You + Text = Response

An equation? Are you sure you're not a Maths examiner as well in your spare time?

No. But I do enjoy dressing up as a pink emu and taking part in re-enactments of the Battle of Hastings on summer weekends.

Quite. Well, thank you very much. And don't worry. The men in white coats will be here soon…

Seriously, as you write your exam answer there are FIVE questions that you should constantly be asking yourself:

● Am I answering the question?
● Am I proving that I know the text – that I've read it?
● Am I showing that I understand it?
● Am I looking at language, and minding my own?
● Am I giving my own response to the text?

If you can honestly say you're doing all of these, then a good grade is guaranteed.

And when the two or two-and-a-half hours are up, and your arm is aching from writing at speed, and your brain is still in overdrive, you can take a few deep breaths and relax. Your only problem now is what to do with all your spare time now your Eng Lit exam is over.

That's not a problem. As soon as GCSEs are over I'm off on holiday with my mates. Then I'm catching up with what I've missed on the box, and just enjoying having nothing to do at all. And then, at the end of August – Omigod! It's results day! Aaargh!!

If you take the advice in this book, you won't be dreading results day. Far from it. If I were you, I'd start planning your celebration right now.

Cool! I will. And then I think I might just read this book through again...

And finally, folks...

6

It's true that English Literature can sometimes seem intimidating. It's even more true that exams on English Literature can seem doubly intimidating. But that's only an illusion, as much as Macbeth's dagger. Just remember...

- You *will* understand your set text – your teachers will help you, and it's amazing how things click on a second, or third reading.

- Literature is easier to learn than many other GCSE subjects as most of it is concerned with stories, and stories make sense.

- Writing about literature is a matter of applying common sense. If you think and write clearly and logically you won't go far wrong.

- Finding things to say about your set text will become second nature by the end of your GCSE course.

- If you know your texts, once you're in the examination room your knowledge plus the rush of adrenalin you'll get will ensure your success.

Literary terms

And now, in handy reference form for calming those last-minute nerves, here's a glossary of the technical terms used in this book with quick definitions:

Alliteration — words close to each other beginning with the same sound.

Character sketch — the main points about a character with evidence.

Compare and contrast — finding things two texts have in common, and things that are different about them.

Diction — a writer's choice of words.

Dramatic irony — when the audience or reader knows more about the situation the characters are in than the characters themselves.

Empathetic writing — writing as if you are a character in the text.

End-stopped line — a line of poetry that ends with a full stop.

Free verse — a poem with no regular rhyme or rhythm.

Iambic pentameter — ten syllables in every line, generally following the pattern short syllable–long syllable, short syllable–long syllable, etc.

Imagery — comparisons — similes and metaphors.

Irony — when a writer writes one thing but means the opposite.

Metaphor — a comparison that doesn't use "like" or "as".

Narrative viewpoint — whose point of view the story is told from, e.g. a character's, or the author's.

Novel – a long, continuous work of prose fiction.

Onomatopoeia – when a word sounds like its meaning.

Pathetic fallacy – when something inanimate such as the weather matches the mood of a passage or character.

Personification – describing something as if it was a person.

Plot – the story which explains *why* things happen.

Prose – anything not written in poetry, continuous sentences divided into paragraphs.

Rhyming couplet – two lines of poetry next to each other that rhyme.

Simile – a comparison using "like" or "as".

Sonnet – a poem with 14 lines.

Stanza – a verse of a poem – a better word to use than verse!

Theme – a recurring idea in the text explored in various ways by the author.

So now you know, and you're ready to tackle your English Literature GCSE.
    And you won't go wrong as long as you remember to...
- Be sensitive.
- Be confident.
- Have fun.
- Keep this book nearby for handy reference!

198

Answers

Oh no! Things are getting critical!
Page 42
1. He's rich – he has "ten thousand a year"
2. People admire him to begin with – the gentlemen said he was "a fine figure of a man", the ladies said he was "handsomer than Mr Bingley" and "he was looked at with great admiration for about half the evening".
3. He's proud (or possibly shy) – he only dances with and speaks to the people he came with.

Page 42
Dill is small for his age – "he wasn't much higher than the collards" and "You look right puny for goin' on seven".
He's boastful, a big talker – "I'm Charles Baker Harris... I can read." and "You got anything needs readin' I can do it"
He can stick up for himself – "I'm little but I'm old."

How does that writer do it?
Page 55
positives = willowy, slender, slim; negatives = lanky, bony, skeletal

Page 64
1. Short **2.** Long **3.** Short **4.** Long **5.** Short **6.** Short

Page 68
The best answers are **1b)**, **2c)**, **3d)**, **4a)**.

Page 99
You should have picked **b)**, **c)** and **e)**.

Plays, prose, poetry... read all about it!
Page 125
1. a) Free verse. (Blank verse, by the way, has a regular rhythm, often ten syllables per line.)
2. c) Couplet – just like a couple has two people in it.
3. c) Stanza – most people think verse is OK, but you should only use the word "verse" when you're talking about a song.
4. b) End-stopped (which is logical). When no punctuation mark separates a line of poetry from the next, it's called enjambement.
5. d) A Sonnet. (A limerick has five lines, rhyme scheme a, a, b, b, a.)

5 correct – Poet Laureate!
4 correct – You're a poet and you didn't know it.
3 correct – You could do verse.
2, 1 or none correct – Try the quiz again!

How do I write right in English?
Page 161
The slang words are **1b)** totally **2a)** wicked **3b)** dead.

Page 169
How did you do? Here are some alternative versions:

1. Lady Macbeth will do anything to get to the top.
2. Atticus Finch never boasts about being a good lawyer.

3. Napoleon loves power and will use others so that he can keep it.
4. Although the story of "The Lady of Shalott" is sad, ending with the death of the heroine, the poetry is beautiful, having the haunting rhythms of a song.

Acknowledgements

Extracts from the following are reproduced with the kind permission of:

The Random House Group: *To Kill a Mockingbird* © Harper Lee,
published by William Heinemann.

David Higham Associates: "The Destructors" from *Collected Stories*
© Graham Greene, published by Random House.

John Murray (Publishers) Ltd: "Slough" from *Collected Poems* © John Betjeman,
published by John Murray (Publishers) Ltd.

Faber and Faber: "Afternoons" from *Collected Poems* © Philip Larkin,
"The Jaguar" from *The Hawk in the Rain* © Ted Hughes, and "Twelve Songs IX"
from *Collected Poems* © W H Auden, published by Faber and Faber.